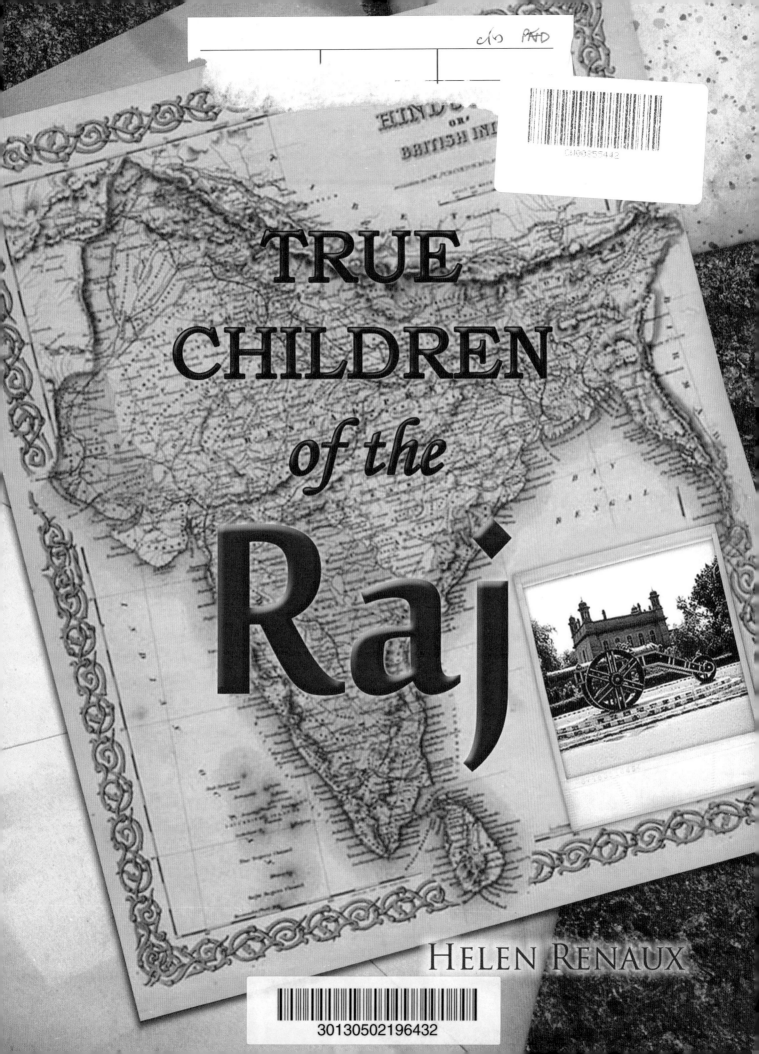

TRUE
CHILDREN
of the
Raj

HELEN RENAUX

 www.trafford.com

North America & international
toll-free: 1 888 232 4444 (USA & Canada)
phone: 250 383 6864 ♦ fax: 812 355 4082

THE TRUE CHILDREN OF THE RAJ

By Helen Renaux

Letters to my grandchildren

An epistolary manuscript about our family history and heritage

Acknowledgements

I wish to convey my grateful thanks to my grandson, Oliver, for making the publishing of this book possible. Thanks too to all my grandchildren, Ben, Rebecca, Emma, Oliver, Jamie, Joshua, Rianna, Luke and Clémentine and my children, Roger, Lorraine, Diane and Caryl for encouraging me to complete this manuscript which started about ten years ago simply as 'letters to my grandchildren' and developed from there onwards to this finished book. I also thank my grandson, Ben, for his ideas in designing the cover and Emma for editing the first draft several years ago and all my family members.

Many thanks too to my friends and acquaintances in UK and all over the world who have encouraged the writing of this book and to my University colleagues and friends who gave me the confidence and the will to complete it and publish it.

I would like to enter a special thank you to my very special friend, Lisa, who persisted in pushing me to complete this book and thanks to Terry, my husband for all his help and patience during the time I spent on writing this book.

I extend my thanks to my publishers and especially to Nick Arden, my personal Publishing Services Consultant at Trafford and the Design Team, for their patience and help with the many changes and amendments I made during the process of publishing.

Helen Renaux

Carpe Diem! Rejoice while you are alive; enjoy the day, live life to the fullest; make the most of what you have.'

Anonymous

A Family History

Introduction

My dearest Grandchildren

I am writing this in the evening of my life in order for you to have a memoir that you and your offspring can refer to when you grow older and become more curious about who you are. Whilst one is young this curiosity is not really a conscious thought. One is extrovert in youth; busy finding out about other, more interesting aspects of life. But as one grows older (I don't mean old like me – just old enough to have acquired wisdom of a sort); when one seems to start to wonder and be curious of one's heritage and identity, then ancestry becomes an important issue. It is for this part of your life that I want to chronicle some important facts of your family background and the life and ways of your ancestors.

As I am your loving grandmother I would like you to have this manuscript, in epistolary format, to read at your leisure. I hope you find it interesting; in some parts, amusing, but most of all the contents of this is a part of your heritage goes towards making you who you are today.

Family is an important unit; one that is there when you are in trouble and in times of grief and despair. It is a bond of blood. Perhaps not through choice, but bound together through love and genetic ties.

Some find us as a family, when we are all together, rather intimidating! We are self assured; some would even call us arrogant! But we are a happy lot; full of quick witted humour, love, outgoing, a bit loud and 'in your face' as the cliché says – perhaps too much for the timid, but we do invite people into our inner circle. Our hearts and our homes are open to those who wish to join us

We are a close knit, self contained group and what is more, we celebrate being together. Some people fit in perfectly with us and thoroughly enjoy our togetherness. They fit in because they accept us for who we are. There are many that have remained within our close knit circle for many years and have become almost a part of our family. One would tend to see the same faces attending our functions; some that have been with our family since they were children. There are those, acquired along life's highways that have become almost as close as real family and there are many dear friends who we cherish. Sadly for some however; and there are the odd few; that seem to feel threatened by our very exuberance and opt to stay on the outside.

As a family group, we are not about to change the way we are. I personally think we are lucky to have each other and to bond the way we do. Of course there are dramatics and upheavals, but that is the way with close knit, strong minded people.

Our strength of personality is deeply ingrained in the roots in our family genes as you will see when reading through this manuscript of family history; the parts of which I have knowledge. There are other branches to your family too and if you need history of those branch lines you will have to trace these for yourselves through the members of those branches. I can only give you information from one side of your family history.

So my darling grandchildren, be happy and proud to be members of this very special group of persons who have been united and tied into a family unit; a unit where all of you, and your extended partners and family, belong and are loved and cherished.

As you are in part the second generation of the Diaspora of the subcontinent of India, I feel that this compilation of family stories, historical information might enlighten you and those that follow after you as a personal history of our family and the culture that formed us.

I will endeavour to give you a *dénouement* of your ethic origins, which I might add, in your case are extremely diluted as there is much of the West in you and much less of the East. However, genes are strong and come through to you from your ancestors (in both halves of your make up) in various ways. I will concentrate by the half that I know about.

During the days of the British and European colonisation of many countries of the world, a hybrid race of people was created by intermarriage or cohabitation of the colonisers and the colonised. Being of mixed blood was not that important an issue for me personally in India; a country that I am familiar with and can write about. We, that is so called Anglo Indians, had our own culture, neither British nor Indian even though we were more British than Indian. Generally speaking, the British as a norm had a high and mighty outlook and considered themselves to be the 'superior' race. In hindsight they had the power and power is an all important issue. British Imperialism spread world wide and if one looks at the size of Britain in comparison to the countries they colonised, one has but to admire their amazing strength of sea and manipulative power.

India is a huge country with millions of people, but the British needed a go-between race to help them rule the colonised peoples of India. This idea was not initially in their heads as far as I know, but time and circumstances happened and the idea generated interesting thinking. This hybrid race of people were already being formed when Britain decided it was a good idea to have this Anglo-Indian mix and they actually encouraged British men to have children with Indian women. They paid fifteen silver rupees as an allowance for each child born to these couples. The result of course was that there were many large families. Each couple producing up to and above ten children! In the 1700 to 1800's 15 silver rupees was a great deal of money. It was an incentive to procreate and many a marriage was formed. There were some children who were born out of wedlock. Some of these unfortunate children were disowned by the father and were put into orphanages because the mothers were full time workers; usually in tea plantations. However, as far as I can ascertain, the allowance was paid to married couples only.

Since this is a manuscript of information for you, I think a little matter of identity, ethnicity and form filling needs to be addressed.

This has always been a bit complicated for most of us, but I notice some of you are a little confused as to your ethnicity.

Let me therefore enlighten you as to your national identity as it is today. Your nationality is British, or in the case of Clementine, British or French. She has dual nationality. Because your origins are mixed, on some forms there is a stipulation to list an ethnic background. You should select the heading of 'other' if there is such an option; if not just ignore the ethnicity choice entirely. You are not Asian, not Pakistani, not Indian, not Jamaican and not French. You do not fit into these broad categories of ethnicity. What is on your passport is your proper 'nationality'. Your 'ethnic background' is eclectic.

Since I am now living in the United Kingdom, with a British Passport as a British citizen, perhaps I should feel guilty writing my opinions publicly about the British in India. I do not. Facts are facts and there was a time when Britain was an Imperialistic Power and did spread their genes indiscriminately around the world. They were young men, without any women of their own kind in a foreign land, surrounding by beautiful women of the countries they colonised and these couplings were predestined to happen.

I am sure that many English people today, who read of the history of the 'Raj' for instance, find it difficult to understand how Britain appropriated so much wealth from India and serfdom from its people. India was known as the jewel in the crown.

If one looks back in history, the ancestral genealogy of most people in the world is a mixture somewhere of some other race or culture. This mixing of blood and genes mostly occurred because of wars and countries being conquered. Even aristocracy in Britain, as in various parts of the world, is of mixed race!

Europe itself in ancient times was a mishmash of barbaric peoples. In the seventeenth century, British missionaries went to India, with the merchants, the East India Company, to help 'civilise' the natives; teach them how to think and to bring them 'into the fold' as it were. The irony of this misconception is apparent.

India had civilisations in the Bronze Age (3300—1300 BCE), for instance, with plumbing, underwater heating systems etc in the Indus Valley Civilisation, one of the oldest civilisations in the world. This civilisation was located in the northern regions of the Indian sub continent (now Pakistan). It is also known as the Harappan Civilisation. There were other civilisations all over India as will be seen by the little chart I have inserted further on in this manuscript. Europe during this period (3300 BCE) was surely still barbaric. After the Romans occupied and colonised most of Europe, many battles were fought between the well armed Romans and the stone weaponry of the 'barbarians' so I have read and after many years, areas were conquered by Rome. Over a long period of time, we eventually had countries like France, Germany, and England etc. I am not too well versed in European history, because I was always interested specifically in English and Indian history and those were my main study subjects. Please do not quote me on European history as I have not studied it in detail; I just have general knowledge of the subject.

India was invaded by the Aryans, the Greeks (Alexander the Great, Genghis Khan, two for example) and many others. India was always a country that was sort after for its wealth of jewels, its gold and silver mines, spices, and its lush and arable land. Even Shakespeare in the 1500's uses an analogy about India's wealth as quoted below.

Henry IV, Part I, Act 3, scene 1
MORTIMER:
In faith, he is a worthy gentleman . . .
. . . wondrous affable, and as bountiful as mines of India.

I re-track back to our lineage and mixed genes. I am part French, part English, part Portuguese, and part Indian. Noel, your granddad who died before any of you were born, had Scottish and English on his father's side; Louisa's (your G/Grandmother) had Irish on her father's side. She was christened Louisa, but most people called her Louise. There was the inevitable Indian mixed in there somewhere. That is some mixture of genes! 'Anglo Indian' used as an ethnic race and still used today, is actually quite an oblique term. Its origin was concocted and used by the British who domiciled in India, and then the term was transferred to the hybrid race that they created; British/Indian. In our case the word meant that the male line had to be English. Rudyard Kipling's quote

'East is East and West is West and never the twain shall meet
Till Earth and Sky stand presently by God's great Judgement Seat'

turned out to be a misleading notion. With all due respect to the great man and his works, this particular statement was a totally erroneous belief. As far as our ethnicity is concerned, East and West met, married or cohabited in India (and other colonised countries) and produced offspring.

Eastern cultures, and others too, have come to the West and have mixed and mingled here, making UK a cosmopolitan country; similar to Canada, the United States and Australia. The resulting off spring of these unions as it happens turn out to be of a beautiful aspect. It appeared that the East and West combination of genes actually brought out the best of both worlds, physically and intellectually. For some reason the mixture of blood lines enhanced beauty and enriched the genes of the off spring.

We see today a mixture of Caribbean/English, Asian/English and Indian/English. Take a look at the children. The majority turn out to be very attractive. Again it is the blending of these different blood lines that seem to bring out this beauty in the genetic mix. Most of the so called Anglo Indians were also better at all forms of sport; physically sturdy and fit. I have not studied any of this scientifically I just see it as an observer. It is something to look into and ascertain why and how.

It is probably because of this gene mixture that the author Jean Rhys in 'Wide Sargasso Sea' took up the case of Bertha Mason of Jane Eyre fame; the mad wife in the attic. Jean Rhys was Creole as Bertha Mason was characterised to be in Charlotte Bronte's novel. Rhys empathised with the character of Bertha Mason and took umbrage at the racist comments in Jane Eyre's book. Rhys wrote her book from Bertha's point of view. Wide Sargasso Sea was a work of fiction, as was Jane Eyre, but it too had colonial issues. Rhys used the fact that the character she based on Rochester of Jane Eyre, married Antoinette (Wide Sargasso Sea) (who was in turn based on Bertha) for her wealth and beauty. Rochester was characterised to marry Antoinette to enrich his status in England as he was the younger son and would not inherit his father's estate. Again we are faced with Colonial usage here. Wide Sargasso Sea is a romantic but tragic story. Read it if you can. It was also a play made famous as The Last Mrs Rochester.

Below is a gist of the play, the main character in it is an acquaintance of mine, Diana Quick. I thoroughly enjoyed the powerful performance of Diana as Jean Rhys and Bertha. It was a very clever play based on a great novel. The reason I add this is because it is partly based on the result of colonialism, the subject I am covering in this manuscript. I think you would really enjoy the novel. The play unfortunately is now closed. I loved it. The book is available and topical to what I am writing about in this manuscript.

Below is a synopsis of the play. You will see why I relate it to my writing. Rhys, however, though a brilliant writer and very talented, was paranoid about her mixed blood. She had an identity crises which caused havoc in her life.

After Mrs Rochester
By Polly Teale
Duke of York's Theatre
16 July—1 Nov 2003

Jean Rhys is best known for her novel *The Wide Sargasso Sea*, the story of the first Mrs Rochester who ends up as a mad woman in the attic in Charlotte Bronte's *Jane Eyre*. Jean Rhys was fascinated with this underdeveloped character from an early age in part because she herself had a similar background. Born in Dominica she was a white Creole who was torn between feeling advantaged on the one hand and on the other being derided for being a 'white nigger'.

Polly Teale's play, *After Mrs Rochester* is a wonderful examination of Jean Rhys's life, her struggle for identity and the demons who tormented her, whether real, like her mother and the men who loved and then abandoned her, or imagined, as in her characters, Mrs Rochester in particular.

Diana Quick is the older Rhys, locked in her room and refusing to open the door to her daughter, glugging gin from the bottle and reliving her past, while Mrs Rochester is an ever-present being, almost becoming one with Rhys at times. Madeleine Potter plays the younger Rhys full of fire and spirit trying to make sense of her life and finally at quite a late stage learning to cope by writing about it. Both women are excellent, playing off one another and remaining at the same time two parts of a whole. Towards the end the older Rhys says to the younger, 'When you've written it, it doesn't hurt anymore.' If only we all had our older selves to advise us in our youth!

The locked room is a beautiful metaphor for Rhys's mind, the characters from her past, including Jane Eyre and Mr Rochester, appearing and disappearing as her life unwinds before us. She cannot escape them and at the same time she could not live without them. She refuses to let her daughter enter, mirroring her incapability of being a mother to her. Having given her up as a baby she tried when she was eight to develop a relationship but failed miserably. And yet her daughter is here, begging to be let in and in the final moments of the play, having in a sense dealt with her demons, Rhys does open the door to her.

Syan Blake and Amy Marston stand out in a cast where the acting is universally good, both playing numerous characters. They are particularly effective as Rhys's childhood friend and her daughter respectively. Rhys says of Tite, her friend from the West Indies, that she never saw her sad and Blake effortlessly conveys a spirit full of adventure and cheekiness. Marston, whether playing an eight-year-old, Jane Eyre, or a snooty shop assistant, is a delight to watch.

There are some brilliant moments such as when we see Jane Eyre's Mrs Rochester attacking her husband, while Jane looks on and at the same time the young Rhys attacking her lover who is about to leave her as Diana Quick observes all from the back, in control of chaos. The magical thing is that none of it is confusing or inappropriate. When Rhys's daughter is finally let in the room she asks her mother whether she would have preferred to have been happy or to have been a writer. The question doesn't need an answer—she had no choice. And Polly Teale's play is a fitting tribute to this tortured but hugely talented woman.

Francine Brody

Strangely, the actress Diana Quick felt a connection with India as her ancestors lived there. The tug was strong and so she travelled to India, Pakistan and Afghanistan. She is a highly successful actress on screen and stage, but somehow she found time to research resolutely and eventually found her Indian ancestry. At one time Diana asked me to take part in a documentary she was making on the subject of India. Her book is very aptly entitled *A Tug on the Thread.* **I highly recommend it for historical and factual information about the British in India. I really enjoyed the book. Her efforts eventually helped her find her Indian connection.**

Yours, my darling grandchildren, is an exotic and unique heritage. The genealogical history of part of your family roots, belong in the great sub-continent of India where our particular culture was created by the British and Europeans during their colonisation of India for over 200 years, commonly known as the 'British Raj'. We were in fact the true children of the Raj. There are books and television documentaries entitled 'The Children of the Raj' but they are children of the English colonisers of India. Their stay was limited and in 1947 they were forced to leave India.

This document is primarily to give you a 'peep' into your genetic and historic background through those of your ancestors on mine and your Granddad Noel's side of the family. This history I might add is exciting and different to the norm and I would love you to have knowledge of it. The other half of your heritage lies here in the United Kingdom.

It would be sad not to enlighten you on your uniqueness in this side of your lineage. If I do not write this down for you it would be lost in time as our (mine and your Granddad's) cultural background is fading fast and therefore you will have no exotic tales to pass on to your children and grandchildren in their time because this little bit of history that makes you so special will be lost forever. We are a disappearing race.

The gathered facts in my narrative have been gleaned from various sources; some from my grandparents, parents, genealogical research; some that I learned in school, both socially and literally and what I myself have experienced through living in India/Pakistan until September 1962 to the age of 36. This last 'primary source' is the most reliable source of our personal history.

Before I take you on a journey into the past I would like to leave a few of my philosophies with you. I do not intend this as a lecture; let us say it is more a passing on of experience from grandmother to grandchildren.

At eighty five I think I have acquired certain experiences of life but I do not profess in any way to think I know all the answers. I certainly do not. Life is a journey in which we continue to learn, no matter how old we may be. I personally do not enjoy living in the past, even though I treasure my memories, I like to live in the present. I have found many old people who wallow in their past lives and seem to miss all that is happening in the ever changing and exciting world of today. Life, to my way of thinking, is all progress and I believe one must move with the times.

However for this narrative I am delving into the past, but it is for a purpose of information for you, not as a journey of nostalgia for me. However, I might very well feel nostalgia as I write and remember.

These are my philosophical journeys and contain my personal assessments. Each of you, however, must take and live your own journey and form your own ideas in life and learn its lessons through your personal experiences.

It is common knowledge that the mind controls the body; what you *think* is what you *are.* This philosophy works in whatever way you want it to therefore make good use of the power of thought. Use it as a tool. I am a strong believer in the old adage, 'mind over matter'. I don't like writing metaphors or clichés, but I will let this one ride. It is apt. I also believe and know that one has control of one's own destiny. No matter what happens in your particular lives it is you that hold the reigns and you that make the choices. If you encounter adversity treat it as a teacher; it strengthens the character. Do not envy others' success or riches. It is futile and a waste of your time; rather put in effort to achieve your own status in life. Self pity and envy are not options and should never be indulged. Money is not the only asset to aspire to; there are many other much worthier and fulfilling aspirations to aim for.

It is inspiring to keep challenging yourself. Personal challenges keep your mind and body occupied and help you to be positive. Always aim a little higher than your aspirations. The challenge is the prop that keeps you going and I hope you never lose the desire to aim for the highest rung of the ladder within your particular choices. Not just to be successful; not just to be an achiever (though these are wonderful aims) but because you have it in you to do better than you consciously realise. We all have this ability but we do not tap the source that provides the power. This source is within you.

As you know I love anything that is different! Graduating with two degrees; one at age eighty two, and then on to an Honours degree in Literature at age eighty three was tough and a monstrous challenge. The brain of an octogenarian is supposed to be worn out, so most people believe. I do not think it, nor do I believe it, and hence I obtained my dream. Everyone can see very clearly that I do not look, nor do I feel as old as I am. I am always being asked what my secret is. I really do not have a secret. Once again I believe everything in life is controlled by thought pattern. I am excited about life and all the new developments and discoveries of science. I live my life at full tilt. I always have a project in tow. I love people and I live in the present. So my darling grandchildren perhaps this is my secret. You too can achieve amazing aims if you believe in yourself and think outside of the general norm.

Here then, my darlings, is my story, the story of your parents, before you knew them, your grandparents and our ancestors. Also included in this manuscript is a short geographical and historical background of India and Pakistan described to the best of my personal knowledge; the two countries that are a part of your heritage. I have included this knowledge for you to realise the kind of background that is a part of your roots.

The sub-continent of India is a fascinating country and I would love you to know of its amazing and colourful history. As mentioned earlier in this narrative, India was a highly civilised country centuries ago, when Britain and parts of Europe was still **uncivilised**. India, and now Pakistan, is also topographically and geographically beautiful and varied. There exist **most** of the highest mountains in the world, vast deserts, arid plains and green and fertile land. It is a country of contrast, bright colours and diversity in its population.

Writing about your parents as children and young adults and of our early years in England before you were born may be amusing and informative for you I feel. It was transference of cultures from East to West which in itself was a momentous upheaval for your granddad and me and our children, your parents, aged seven, five, three and one at that time.

We were actually brought up in India within an English permeated society and English was our way of life, but it took place in the East where Eastern culture was bound to infringe. My children, however, having developed in England grew up knowing no other culture but that of the West. When they first arrived in England, they too missed some of the luxuries and the ways of the East. They missed their servants and their ayahs (nannies) who played a big part in their young lives. Roger and Lorraine missed their schools. It was a difficult transition for them and far more for us, their parents. They soon forgot their eastern life style and adapted quickly to the west.

People in this country find it difficult to understand that we had servants. Many of my friends refer to them as slaves. Well our servants were a part of our family life. They loved being with us and we loved having them. In no way whatsoever were they treated as slaves. Yes, they worked for a wage and worked for us, but their lives were totally intertwined with ours. It was a way of life in the East.

There are visuals appended within this manuscript for you to look at and to help you take in what I am showing you of your ancestry and of the land where it all began. Keep these pictures. Future generations may find them of interest.

I read somewhere a passage that struck me as relevant to any writer, 'A story is a letter an author writes to himself, to tell himself things that he would be unable to discover otherwise.' ('*Shadow of the Wind' by Carlos Ruiz Zafon.)* So perhaps these are letters I am writing for myself to open up my memory store and thus to convey these memories to you, and in so doing enlighten all of us.

When one thinks one creates pictures and dreams, but when one attempts to recollect and 'discover' the past one probes the depths of mind, both conscious and subconscious. As one writes, memories come flooding in; such as things one might have forgotten or put to the back of one's mind whilst rushing around getting through the daily routine of living. What joy some authors give to others by the sharing of their discoveries, mostly based on experience, in the telling and showing in their stories! This is what I find when I read. No matter what the genre, fiction, life writing, poetry or what ever one chooses to use in the book field, the author's self is revealed within the lines of the narrative. How can one write about feeling something without having experienced it for oneself? Of course one can imagine, but I feel certain that experience is the ultimate grounding for any narrative. I hope you will find this manuscript interesting.

So, my darlings, let's step back in time to see
And try to use chronology
How these events of history
Made them and you and me
And those that follow in our family tree.

Chapter One

Your Grandparents on one side of your ancestry

Good morning my darlings

Bear with me today. I opened this document to continue with my manuscript of your heritage but I feel poetic so I am going to write how I feel. All of you know of your grandmother's whims and fancies and determined ways.

Early morning writing is a task for every writer and this is a self dialogue on the subject! I am about to do some writing on my manuscript but I am not in the mood right now, so you can read this instead! Incidentally I broke most of the rules of poetry. I choose my right to poetic license.

Procrastination

Curled into the foetal position
Waking up in the early morning haze.
Does one have to get up and write?
Right now?
At this early hour of the day?
I say,' no';
Rather lie here and dream, and gaze
At the ceiling than pick up a note book and pen.
One's not in the mood.

No, no, that's not the rule of an author, a poet—
Write—write anything. Look out of the window.
Be creative; be aware of things, like fresh air,
Rustling trees in the wind with leaves autumnal
In colours, red, orange, gold.
Be bold.
At this time of the morning?
Not likely!

Yes, pick up a note book, with a page that is blank
Scribble or scrawl on it words, any words.
Hold on to the pad now, don't put it down now—
Start writing.

No, just a minute. First coffee—
Caffeine's good for the mind.
Kettle starts boiling; pour into the café tier

Aroma exhilarating now fills the air.
Nose starts twitching,
Waiting to taste; to sip the
Morning elixir.

Sipping, enjoying this first 'hit' of the day
Coffee's so good now, mind's fully aware.
Now one can write.
Pick up the note book, pick up the pen
But wait – mind's blank – oh dear!
What now?

Look at the blank page fill it with words, any words.
Words of awareness, description and such
Just write poems. Alliterate, assonate, rhyme.
Describe the morning it shouldn't take much—
Write now!

Listen to the birdsong; look at dew on the leaves
Glistening and twinkling, then dropping.
Smell the fresh grass of the morning,
Dampened with dew drops
Or just say what you're doing
Right now.

Oh dear!
Procrastination's destroyed it;
One's waited too long
One's broken the mood.
Oh, what a pity, it's lost for today. Still,
There's always tomorrow, another new day,
And then one can do it.
Write then!

This is tomorrow so here continues manuscript writing!

As the author of this manuscript it is important, I think, to tell you a little about me and my family; how and where I originated from and the course my life took to bring me to this time of being your grandmother. This is not an actual autobiography, but a document of genealogy and family history.

I was born in a military town named Ferozepore, India, in 1925, first child to Percival and Daisy. I do not remember this part of my life so I pen here what my mother told me. My Dad named me 'Norma' after the Opera *Norma* by Vincenzo Bellini. *Norma* was the High Priestess of the Druidical Temple of Esus. It is an opera of high drama, love and sacrifice. My Dad, like me, was a lover of the Arts; literature and drama. Perhaps that is why I am commonly called by my family, 'drama queen!' I love drama in all its aspects so I do not really mind the title.

My cultural background was Anglo-Indian. I would prefer to use the term Eurasian because our make up was not just English/Indian. On my father's side the family was mostly English Army Officers with one such marrying an Indian girl. Well, we like to think she is Indian but the records are not specific enough. On my mother's side of the family there is French, Portuguese, English and again somewhere, Indian.

The women of India are beautiful; they walk with elegance and were a temptation to the men who had no women in their lives in the early days of colonization. Most of the off spring were born in wedlock; some out of it. We are the product of these connections.

In my case however, my lineage can be traced back on the my father's side to many high ranking officers in the British Army; one such being General Palmer who served with Warren Hastings in the 1800's. He married a very rich and noble Princess, called Faiz or Fyze (a nick name I think). Below is information on General William Palmer and a picture of the family painted by the famous painter Johann Zoffany. One of William's children, John Palmer (*(The Richest East India Merchant) a book by* the Historian Anthony Webster (which I have) married Mary Sarah Hampton who is the sister of my G/G grandfather's wife, Sarah Hampton Middlecoat. Therefore their off spring is blood related to me and thereby to you. John Palmer was very rich as the book's title tells. Unfortunately he was not the son of Princess Fyze but was by General William and his first wife, Sarah Hazlet, a Creole who would not come to India with her husband and so they mutually agreed a divorce. She was from St Kitts and wished to remain there.

Princess Fyze was a direct descendant to the Emperor Shah Jahan, the builder of the world famous Taj Mahal! Unfortunately, she was a loving step mother to our ancestor and so we have no claim to being connected with a blood line to the famous Shah Jahan and the Taj Mahal, but there is a marital connection through the General.

Is this not romantic enough?

See below a picture of the General and Fyze, the Mughal Princess, with their family. Fyze brought John Palmer up as a child as his father took him to India after the divorce.

The Palmer Family

A relation to William Palmer, <u>Richard Palmer</u> offers an alternative interpretation:

The painting is not by Renaldi, but is by Zoffany and is unfinished. It was probably painted at Lucknow. The original is in the India Office in London, having been purchased by them in 1925. The lady on my Great, Great, Great Grandfather's left is his sister-in-law. General William Palmer (b. 1740 - d. 1816) was, in the early days of his career in India, confidential secretary to Warren Hastings; and Political Agent in Gwalior, 1791 - 94. He married, (in 1779) Fyze Baksh, (d. 1828) a princess of the Royal House of Delhi, and a descendant of the Shah Jahan, the builder of the Taj Mahal. The Princess is the lady on his right. The other three

Reading the little note below the picture is quite thrilling for me (and I hope for you) to know that in our ancestral line, there is a tiny link to the Emperor Shah Jahan and his famous monument, the Taj Mahal! The Princess is the lady with the baby. It is a romantic story even if the relationship is only through marriage and not a direct blood tie as such; I still think I should include this item in my manuscript.

Another of our direct ancestors is Nicholas Middlecoat (Junior) my three times great grandfather, who was quite a famous personage in Cornwall, where the Middlecoat family came from. I managed to get hold of a book he wrote in 1796. It is a study book on Social Sciences and is written in Old English. I append below a copy of the cover. Nicholas was a political agent; also a private tutor who enjoyed teaching rather than doing it for a living. Similar to this book I am writing, Nicholas' book is in epistolary format.

Social Sciences

Answer to an address, dated St. James's Square, 16th. March 1796, and signed Richard Barwell. By Nicholas Middlecoat.

Nicholas Middlecoat

Nicholas portrayed giving private tuition to children.

Nicholas portrayed giving private tuition to children.

Nicholas was accused of bribery by Barwell to collect votes for his candidate and this book is one in which he vindicates himself of all blame.

Anglo Indians are an exceptional race of people who chartered their own way of life; their own culture because circumstances of inheritance made us 'other'. Yes we were 'other'. We had European blood in our veins which made us different to the Indian natives and again different to the Europeans because we also had Indian blood. We were a mixture of both and I personally think we had the best of both worlds.

The British placed us on pedestals by giving us excellent educational facilities; the cream jobs because they needed us as a barrier between themselves and the Indians they attempted to rule, thereby instilling a sense of superiority into our psyche. The Anglo Indians, by that very mixture of East and West, were physically and mentally well adjusted. We lived at the same standard as the *'sahibs and memsahibs'* (the sirs and madams) of the Raj and in a sense in a superior way. We felt the British were sahibs in India only; they were 'visitors' in India and just very ordinary people in their own land, whereas we were bred and born into this affluent life style and India was our home. However our loyalties were torn between Britain and India. Most Anglo Indians felt more British than Indian because of the way our culture was set. Britain made sure that that was how we looked at ourselves. They needed our loyalty. Indian life glorified the British in many ways.

Because we went to the best schools and were extremely well educated, we were selected for the very best where work and other activities were concerned; for which we must give credit to the British, even though all of this was done to suit their own needs.

When the British left India in 1947 everything changed. Suddenly the Anglo Indians did not belong anywhere. Some opted to stay in India and it seems their lifestyle is now much diminished. The rest of us migrated to other countries. From 1947 onwards there was a mass emigration of Anglo Indians to all parts of the globe.

However, now that our race or culture is fast fading out of existence and since we have been researching our family tree I thought it is time to pass the knowledge of these findings on to you.

The whole picture has to be seen from the inside out and not from the outside in. I mean I was there in the days of the Raj and am witness to what I am writing. Anglo Indians, for lack of a better term, is a dying race as it is being integrated into cultures of the West. In the next millennium 'Anglo Indians' will probably be non-existent in the west anyway. Your parents are British and you certainly are British. You and others of your generation will be incorporated into various American, Australian, British, Canadian and other European cultures.

In my experience, and I can only speak for myself and my knowledge, being Anglo-Indian was a privilege in British India. As I stated earlier we were the true children of the Raj. We evolved within it. We were cosseted by the British; lived an affluent lifestyle, with big houses and many servants. We had good jobs and were considered superior to Indians, which was very much what the British encouraged us to feel, though we were and are a mixture of both races. Not always British/Indian but some of us were a mixture of French, Portuguese or Dutch with an Indian ancestor somewhere in our family tree; a race of mixed bloods. We were colourful, we were interesting and we were unique. We are what one could refer to as an exotic cocktail!

Many of our kind had identity problems; it did not help much when the British referred to us as 'coloured' or half caste and other detrimental names. It was mostly the soldiers and there were many of them and eventually their wives who also considered themselves as the privileged few. They had never had it as good as they did in India.

Speaking for myself, I had no identity problem and the racial prejudice of some of the British did not bother me one iota. I thought too well of myself. I was a happy child, living in a wide open country with no boundaries, and a happy and contented grown up. I had the sort of personality that could not be put down. I was brought up to have a high regard for myself and my own identity, encouraged by my very intellectual father and my gentle mother, who loved everybody. I hope I instilled this concept of self worth into my children. Below are pictures of my parents, your great grandparents and of Noel and me in younger days.

You have probably seen these pictures before but they are here for posterity and for those who follow. There is one of my Mum and one of my Dad. Noel was a wonderful diver and in one picture we are sitting on the high diving board from which he jack-knifed, swallowed, piked and did several other dives. Both Noel and my brother Derrick had competitions in diving. It was the only pool in Lahore suitable for high diving. I often jumped off the high diving board into the pool before I could swim and one of the boys would wait for me to surface and guide me to the side. I could just about doggy paddle. I did learn to swim there eventually. The other picture is of Noel's and my wedding reception and one of Noel.

Before your Granddad I married   *Our wedding day 20 June 1954*

Noel 1953   *Norma 1952*

I, despite being classed as 'Anglo-Indian' with a leaning towards English, loved the musical sound of the language of Urdu and Arabic for that matter. Urdu is a poetic, musical language and I love the artistic script that flows from right to left. Most of the world writes from left to right, I of course preferred the opposite direction; an early indication of my fascination and love for all things different. The script is all curves and it flows. I loved learning it in school and writing it too. Below is the Urdu alphabet but it is so much more picturesque joined in words and sentences. It is a beautiful looking script.

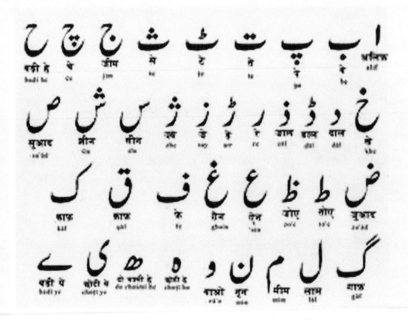

I am fascinated by the sound of voices. Some are profound and thrilling, while some are discordant. However, once, flying in Pakistan on PIA airlines, from Karachi to Islamabad, I heard the customary reciting of a prayer. I think it was a reading from the Koran, but I am not sure. It was begun as soon as the aircraft began its take off and continued right until the cabin crew was allowed to leave their seats, when the aircraft was airborne. The point of this mention is that the voice of the reader was arresting and was the most beautiful speaking voice that I had ever heard. The intonation, the depth and the timbre of his voice gave me goose pimples. Even though I could not understand all of it – it was in pure Arabic I think—I didn't need to know the meaning of the words, because the voice and the sound of the words soothed, comforted and spiritually uplifted me in tandem with the rising of the aircraft from the ground skywards. I felt a presence, being projected by this voice, in that aircraft. It seemed to be speaking to me personally. It was an unusual spiritual experience. I've heard the prayer since but it was that particular voice that had me enthralled. It was an experience that made a lasting impression.

Your speaking voice is very important so try to develop it. Many people judge you by the way you speak, so speak clearly and not too fast; after all you are communicating and the listener has to understand what you say.

As a child I was, and still am, an insatiably curious person. Curiosity towards knowledge is a gift; as it leads you through doorways that some do not think to look into. Nevertheless, that is where you will find the treasure of knowledge and a deep understanding of what makes us humans 'tick'. Curiosity, a constant search for knowledge, love of one's neighbour (metaphorically speaking) and keeping in touch with progressive thinking, keeps one young and active. To this I feel I can attest.

I am not an avid viewer of television but I recorded a documentary on language and discovered in scientific knowledge, that even though we know much about our world, the universe, space and other planets, there is still only a very little known about our human brain. I have always believed the capability of the brain is still to be explored as I feel there is vast undiscovered potential that needs to be tapped.

As far as belief in religion is concerned, I am not sure. I feel 'religions' cause wars and dissention and havoc in the world. In context however it is people that cause the trouble in the way they handle religion. I cannot see why there should be dissention. Most religions believe in an omnipotent being, a God in some form and that we will live again in another existence of sorts.

From my point of view I am intolerant of anyone professing to atheism. It seems to me totally closed minded; however, to each his own. Agnostics I can handle; at least they say they are not sure. I feel one should have an open mind. I guess I am spiritual and I do believe in a presence; be it God or spirit. I believe God exists in mankind, not outside of humanity. This might sound blasphemous to some but it is my belief. Belief and faith is very personal and individual.

Knowledge in any form makes you rich in the values that count. It is good to accept one's heritage as it is part of one. We do not choose our heritage it is just there; a fact of life. What we can choose is how to live and how to love.

I do not have much money, but I have enough love to make me the richest person on earth and I feel privileged to be the recipient of this very precious commodity. It is love that has developed my character from an infant to the present day. I am totally and utterly fulfilled as a human being. I am forever grateful for this gift of love; grateful to my forebears, to my children, to you my grandchildren, to both my husbands and to my friends that I have who give me love to sustain and gratify my reason for living. Without love, the world is an empty place. I am a loving person by nature and give out love and I feel that is why people respond to that giving. I feel deep empathy with my fellow travelers in time. It is my way.

As a young student I loved the study of Indian history. I chose it as one of the subjects for my Senior Cambridge. My peers were a bit shocked by my affinity to the subject, as most of those with Anglo-Indian blood, whose prejudice was ingrained, turned up their noses at all things Indian. But not I . . . there was I, learning Indian History and Urdu, the universal language of India. To become fluent in a foreign language, and to be certain, Urdu was foreign to me, one must use it constantly, and I rarely had the opportunity because I was immersed in an English speaking environment. Even our servants spoke English, as the British influence had already permeated Indian culture. Hence learning Urdu was very difficult, but I persevered and can to this day say quite a bit in Urdu, I can certainly understand it and to some extent read and write a bit and all this by studying it to the age of 17.

I will never regret learning Urdu, but in retrospect, French would certainly have been helpful as I have since travelled to Europe and beyond. Learning French now is difficult but I am persevering. I wish I had the opportunity to speak it constantly with someone fluent in it.

It never entered my head that I would ever leave my beautiful India or Pakistan. I embrace everything about both of these countries; the people, the way of life, the pristine mountains and countryside; all of it. This deep affection remains, through the years when the colonisers had taken their toll of the subcontinent and then left it to total chaos and destruction. When I return from time to time I am saddened to see the poverty, the teeming humanity and seeming chaos that has come from 'independence and progress' but it is early years yet. India and Pakistan wanted independence and Britain had to withdraw. To be fair, one has to admit that even though India's wealth (not only monetary) was appropriated by the colonisers, they left behind a legacy; much that is still treasured today, such as architecture, schools, the railways, communication, policing systems and law; all of which are still the basis of what is followed to this day. The British influence certainly lives on in both countries today.

It seems no matter how downtrodden or poor some of the people of India today appear to be, one can always count on a broad smile. They are happy people.

My visits to Pakistan in 2002 and again in 2006 showed a slightly different picture. There is not quite as much poverty as in India; certainly not in the places that I visited. The people are a bit arrogant, but hospitable beyond description. They are a proud race of people and they are difficult to dominate; as is clearly shown in the history of Afghanistan. Their indomitable spirit and outstanding courage cannot be conquered. The country is a wreck because of the Taliban and the war, but the people still survive and endure through the wreckage.

Below is an insert by William Dalrymple, the world famous historian, written last year in the New Statesman? It is a bit long but we as a family should find it interesting reading, as we have two members involved in the present war there. I hope you will find it informative to read. I certainly did.

Article from the New Statesman by William Dalrymple 2010

In 1843, shortly after his return from Afghanistan, an army chaplain, Reverend G R Gleig, wrote a memoir about the First Anglo-Afghan War, of which he was one of the very few survivors. It was, he wrote, "a war begun for no wise purpose, carried on with a strange mixture of rashness and timidity, brought to a close after suffering and disaster, without much glory attached either to the government which directed, or the great body of troops which waged it. Not one benefit, political or military, has Britain acquired with this war. Our eventual evacuation of the country resembled the retreat of an army defeated."

It is difficult to imagine the current military adventure in Afghanistan ending quite as badly as the First Afghan War, an abortive experiment in Great Game colonialism that slowly descended into what is arguably the greatest military humiliation ever suffered by the west in the Middle East: an entire army of what was then the most powerful military nation in the world utterly routed and destroyed by poorly equipped tribesmen, at the cost of £15m (well over £1bn in modern currency) and more than 40,000 lives. But nearly ten years on from Nato's invasion of Afghanistan, there are increasing signs that Britain's fourth war in the country could end with as few political gains as the first three and, like them, terminate in an embarrassing withdrawal after a humiliating defeat, with Afghanistan yet again left in tribal chaos and quite possibly ruled by the same government that the war was launched to overthrow.

Certainly it is becoming clearer than ever that the once-hated Taliban, far from being swept away by General Stanley McChrystal's surge, are instead regrouping, ready for the final act in the history of Hamid Karzai's western-installed puppet government. The Taliban have now advanced out of their borderland safe havens to the very gates of Kabul and are surrounding the capital, much as the US-backed mujahedin once did to the Soviet-installed regime in the late 1980s. Like a rerun of an old movie, all journeys by non-Afghans out of the capital are once again confined largely to tanks, military convoys and helicopters. The Taliban already control more than 70 per cent of the country, where they collect taxes, enforce the sharia and dispense their usual rough justice. Every month, their sphere of influence increases. According to a recent Pentagon report, Karzai's government has control of only 29 out of 121 key strategic districts.

Just recently, on 17 May, there was a suicide attack on a US convoy in the Dar-ul Aman quarter of Kabul, killing 12 civilians and six American soldiers; the following day, there was a daring five-hour-long grenade and machine-gun assault on the US military headquarters at Bagram Airbase, killing an American contractor and wounding nine soldiers, so bringing the death toll for US armed forces in the country to more than 1,000. Then, over the weekend of 22-23 May, there was a series of rocket, mortar and ground assaults on Kandahar Airbase just as the British ministerial delegation was about to visit it, forcing William Hague and Liam Fox to alter their schedule. Since then, a dozen top Afghan officials have been assassinated in Kandahar, including the city of Kandahar's deputy mayor. On 7 June, the deadliest day for Nato forces in months, ten soldiers were killed. Finally, it appears that the Taliban have regained control of the opium-growing centre of Marjah in Helmand Province, only three months after being driven out by McChrystal's forces amid much gung-ho cheerleading in the US media. Afghanistan is going down.

Already, despite the presence of huge numbers of foreign troops, it is now impossible – or at least extremely foolhardy – for any westerner to walk around the capital, Kabul, without armed guards; it is even more inadvisable to head out of town in any direction except north: the strongly anti-Taliban Panjshir Valley, along with the towns of Mazar-e-Sharif and Herat, are the only safe havens left for westerners in the entire country. In all other directions, travel is possible only in an armed convoy.

This is especially true of the Khord-Kabul and Tezeen passes, immediately to the south of Kabul, where as many as 18,000 British troops were lost in 1842, and which are today again a centre of resistance against perceived foreign occupiers. Aid workers familiar with Afghanistan over several decades say the security situation has never been worse. Ideas much touted only a few years ago that Afghanistan might become a popular tourist destination – a Switzerland of central Asia – now seem to be dreams from a distant age. Lonely Planet's guidebook to Afghanistan, optimistically published in 2005, has not been updated and is now once again out of print.

The present war is following a trajectory that is beginning to feel unsettlingly familiar to students of the Great Game. In 1839, the British invaded Afghanistan on the basis of sexed-up intelligence about a non-existent threat: information about a single Russian envoy to Kabul was manipulated by a group of ambitious and ideologically driven hawks to create a scare – in this case, about a phantom Russian invasion – thus bringing about an unnecessary, expensive and entirely avoidable war.

Initially, the hawks were triumphant – the British conquest proved remarkably easy and bloodless; Kabul was captured within a few weeks as the army of the previous regime melted into the hills, and a pliable monarch, Shah Shuja, was successfully placed on the throne. For a few months the British played cricket, went skating and put on amateur theatricals as if on summer leave in Simla; there were discussions about making Kabul the summer capital of the Raj. Then an insurgency began and that first heady success slowly unravelled, first among the Pashtuns of Kandahar and Helmand Provinces. It slowly gained momentum, moving northwards until it reached Kabul, so making the British occupation impossible to sustain.

What happened next is a warning of how bad things could yet become: a full-scale rebellion against the British broke out in Kabul, and the two most senior British envoys, Sir Alexander Burnes and Sir William Macnaghten, were assassinated, one hacked to death by a mob in the streets, the other stabbed and shot by the resistance leader Wazir Akbar Khan during negotiations. It was on the retreat that followed, on 6 January 1842, that the 18,000 East India Company troops, and maybe half that many again Indian camp followers, were slaughtered by Afghan marksmen waiting in ambush amid the high passes, shot down as they trudged through the icy depths of the Afghan winter. After eight days on the death march, the last 50 survivors made their final stand at the village of Gandamak. As late as the 1970s, fragments of Victorian weaponry and military equipment could be found lying in the screes above the village. Even today, the hill is said to be covered with the bleached bones of the British dead.

One Englishman lived to tell the tale of that last stand (if you discount the fictional survival of Flashman) – an ordinary foot soldier, Thomas Souter, wrapped his regimental colours around him to prevent them being captured, and was taken hostage by the Afghans who assumed that such a colourfully clothed individual must command a high ransom. It is a measure of the increasingly pertinent parallels between the 19th-century war and today's that one of the main NATO bases in Afghanistan was recently named Camp Souter after that survivor.

In the years that followed, the British defeat in Afghanistan became pregnant with symbolism. For the Victorian British, it was the country's greatest imperial disaster of the 19th century. It was exactly a century before another army would be lost, in Singapore in 1942. Yet the retreat from Kabul also became a symbol of gallantry against the odds: William Barnes Wollen's celebrated oil painting The Last Stand of the 44th Regiment at Gundamuck – showing a group of ragged but doggedly determined British soldiers standing encircled behind a porcupine of bayonets, as the Pashtun tribesmen close in – became one of the best-known images of the era, along with Remnants of an Army, Elizabeth Butler's image of the wounded and bleeding army surgeon William Brydon, who had made it through to the safety of Jalalabad, arriving before the city walls on his collapsing nag.

For the Afghans, the British defeat of 1842 became a symbol of freedom from foreign invasion. It is again no accident that the diplomatic quarter of Kabul is named after the general who oversaw the rout of the British in that year: Wazir Akbar Khan.

For south Asians, who provided most of the cannon fodder – the foot soldiers and followers killed on the retreat – the war ironically became a symbol of possibility: although thousands of Indians died on the march, it showed that the British army was not invincible and a well-planned insurgency could force them out. Thus, in 1857, the Indians launched their own anti-colonial uprising, the Great Mutiny (as it is known in Britain) or the first war of independence (as it is known in India), partly inspired by what the Afghans had achieved in 1842.

This destabilising effect on south Asia of the failed war in Afghanistan has a direct parallel in the blowback that is today destabilising Pakistan and the tribal territories of the Federally Administered Tribal Areas (Fata). Here the Pakistani Taliban are once more on the march, rebuilding their presence in Swat, and are now surrounding Peshawar, which is almost daily being rocked by bombs, while outlying groups of Taliban are again spreading their influence into the valleys leading towards Islamabad. Across much of the North-West Frontier Province – roughly a fifth of Pakistan's territory – women have now been forced into the burqa, music has been silenced, barbershops are forbidden to shave beards and more than 125 girls' schools have been blown up or burned down.

A significant proportion of the Peshawar elite, along with the city's musicians, have decamped to the relatively safe and tolerant confines of Lahore and Karachi, while tens of thousands of ordinary people from the surrounding hills of the semi-autonomous Fata tribal belt, and especially the Bajaur Agency (or tribal area), have fled from the conflict zones blasted by US Predator drones and strafed by Pakistani helicopter gunships to the tent camps ringing the provincial capital.

The Fata, it is true, have never been fully under the control of any Pakistani government, and have always been unruly, but the region has been radicalised as never before by the rain of shells and cluster bombs that have caused huge civilian casualties and daily add a stream of angry foot soldiers to the insurgency. Elsewhere in Pakistan, anti-western religious and political extremism continues to flourish, as ever larger numbers of ordinary Pakistanis are driven to fight by corruption, predatory politics and the abuse of power by Pakistan's feudal elite, as well as the military aggression of the drones. Indeed, the ripples of instability lapping out from Afghanistan and Pakistan have reached even New York. When CIA interrogators asked Faisal Shahzad why he tried to let off a car bomb last month in Times Square, he told them of his desire to avenge those "innocent people being hit by drones from above".

The route of the British retreat of 1842 backs on to the mountain range that leads to Tora Bora and the Pakistan border, an area that has always been a Taliban centre. I had been advised not to attempt to visit the area without local protection, and so last month I set off for the mountains in the company of a regional tribal leader who was also a minister in Karzai's government. He is a mountain of a man named Anwar Khan Jegdalek, a former village wrestling champion who made his name as a Hezb-e-Islami mujahedin commander in the jihad against the Soviets in the 1980s.

It was Anwar Khan Jegdalek's ancestors who inflicted some of the worst casualties on the British army of 1842, something he proudly repeated several times as we drove through the same passes. "They forced us to pick up guns to defend our honour," he said. "So we killed every last one of those bastards." None of this, incidentally, has stopped Anwar Khan Jegdalek from sending his family away from Kabul to the greater safety of Northolt, Middlesex.

He drove himself in a huge 4x4, while a pick-up full of heavily armed Afghan bodyguards followed behind. We left Kabul – past the blast walls of the Nato barracks built on the very site of the British cantonment of 170 years ago – and headed down a corkscrewing road into the line of bleak mountain passes that links Kabul with the Khyber Pass.

It is a dramatic and violent landscape: fault lines of crushed and tortured strata groaned and twisted in the gunpowder-coloured rock walls rising on either side of us. Above, the jagged mountain tops were veiled in an ominous cloud of mist. As we drove, Anwar Khan Jegdalek complained bitterly of western treatment of his government. "In the 1980s when we were killing Russians for them, the Americans called us freedom fighters," he muttered, as we descended through the first pass. "Now they just dismiss us as warlords."

At Sorobi, where the mountains debouche into a high-altitude ochre desert dotted with encampments of nomads, we left the main road and headed into Taliban territory. A further five trucks full of Anwar Khan Jegdalek's old mujahedin fighters, all brandishing rocket-propelled grenades and with faces wrapped in keffiyehs, appeared from a side road to escort us.

At the crest of Jegdalek village, on 12 January 1842, 200 frostbitten British soldiers found themselves surrounded by several thousand Pashtun tribesmen. The two highest-ranking British soldiers, General Elphinstone and Brigadier Shelton, went off to negotiate but were taken hostage. Only 50 infantrymen managed to break out under cover of darkness. Our own welcome was, thankfully, somewhat warmer. It was my host's first visit to his home since he had become a minister, and the proud villagers took their old commander on a nostalgia trip through hills smelling of wild thyme and rosemary, and up on to mountainsides carpeted with hollyhocks, mulberries and white poplars. Here, at the top of the surrounding peaks, lay the remains of Anwar Khan Jegdalek's old mujahedin bunkers and entrenchments. Once the tour was completed, the villagers fed us, Mughal style, in an apricot orchard: we sat on carpets under a trellis of vine and pomegranate blossom as course after course of kebabs and mulberry pulao was laid in front of us.

During lunch, as my hosts casually pointed out the various places in the village where the British had been massacred in 1842, I asked them if they saw any parallels between that war and the present situation. "It is exactly the same," said Anwar Khan Jegdalek. "Both times the foreigners have come for their own interests, not for ours. They say, 'We are your friends, we want democracy, we want to help.' But they are lying."

"Whoever comes to Afghanistan, even now, they will face the fate of Burnes, Macnaghten and Dr Brydon," said Mohammad Khan, our host in the village and the owner of the orchard where we were sitting. The names of the fighters of 1842, long forgotten in their home country, were still known here.

"Since the British went, we've had the Russians," said an old man to my right. "We saw them off, too, but not before they bombed many of the houses in the village." He pointed at a ridge of ruined mud-brick houses.

"We are the roof of the world," said Mohammad Khan. "From here, you can control and watch everywhere."

"Afghanistan is like the crossroads for every nation that comes to power," agreed Anwar Khan Jegdalek. "But we do not have the strength to control our own destiny – our fate is always determined by our neighbours. Next, it will be China. This is the last days of the Americans."

I asked if they thought the Taliban would come back. "The Taliban?" said Mohammad Khan. "They are here already! At least after dark. Just over that pass." He pointed in the direction of Gandamak and Tora Bora. "That is where they are strongest."

It was nearly five in the afternoon before the final flaps of nan bread were cleared away, by which time it had become clear that it was too late to head on to the site of the British last stand at Gandamak.

Instead, that evening we went to the relative safety of Jalalabad, where we discovered we'd had a narrow escape: it turned out there had been a huge battle at Gandamak that morning between government forces and a group of villagers supported by the Taliban. The sheer scale and length of the feast had saved us from walking straight into an ambush. The battle had taken place on exactly the site of the British last stand.

The following morning in Jalalabad, we went to a jirga, or assembly of tribal elders, to which the greybeards of Gandamak had come under a flag of truce to discuss what had happened the day before. The story was typical of many I heard about the current government, and revealed how a mixture of corruption, incompetence and insensitivity has helped give an opening for the return of the once-hated Taliban.

As Predator drones took off and landed incessantly at the nearby airfield, the elders related how the previous year government troops had turned up to destroy the opium harvest. The troops promised the villagers full compensation, and were allowed to burn the crops; but the money never turned up. Before the planting season, the villagers again went to Jalalabad and asked the government if they could be provided with assistance to grow other crops. Promises were made; again nothing was delivered. They planted poppy, informing the local authorities that if they again tried to burn the crop, the village would have no option but to resist. When the troops turned up, about the same time as we were arriving at nearby Jegdalek, the villagers were waiting for them, and had called in the local Taliban to assist. In the fighting that followed, nine policemen were killed, six vehicles destroyed and ten police hostages taken.

After the jirga was over, one of the tribal elders came over and we chatted for a while over a glass of green tea. "Last month," he said, "some American officers called us to a hotel in Jalalabad for a meeting. One of them asked me, 'Why do you hate us?' I replied, 'Because you blow down our doors, enter our houses, pull our women by the hair and kick our children. We cannot accept this. We will fight back, and we will break your teeth, and when your teeth are broken you will leave, just as the British left before you. It is just a matter of time.'"

What did he say to that? "He turned to his friend and said, 'If the old men are like this, what will the younger ones be like?' In truth, all the Americans here know that their game is over. It is just their politicians who deny this."

The defeat of the west's latest puppet government on the very same hill of Gandamak where the British came to grief in 1842 made me think, on the way back to Kabul, about the increasingly close parallels between the fix that Nato is in and the one faced by the British 170 years ago.

Now as then, the problem is not hatred of the west, so much as a dislike of foreign troops swaggering around and making themselves odious to the very people they are meant to be helping. On the return journey, as we crawled back up the passes towards Kabul, we got stuck behind a US military convoy of eight Humvees and two armoured personnel carriers in full camouflage, all travelling at less than 20 miles per hour. Despite the slow speed, the troops refused to let any Afghan drivers overtake them, for fear of suicide bombers, and they fired warning shots at any who attempted to do so. By the time we reached the top of the pass two hours later, there were 300 cars and trucks backed up behind the convoy, each one full of Afghans furious at being ordered around in their own country by a group of foreigners. Every day, small incidents of arrogance and insensitivity such as this make the anger grow.

There has always been an absolute refusal by the Afghans to be ruled by foreigners, or to accept any government perceived as being imposed on the country from abroad. Now as then, the puppet ruler installed by the west has proved inadequate to the job. Too weak, unpopular and corrupt to provide security or development, he has been forced to turn on his puppeteers in order to retain even a vestige of legitimacy in the eyes of his people. Recently, Karzai has accused the US, the UK and the UN of orchestrating a fraud in last year's elections, described Nato forces as "an army of occupation", and even threatened to join the Taliban if Washington kept putting pressure on him. Shah Shuja did much the same thing in 1842, towards the end of his rule, and was known to have offered his allegiance and assistance to the insurgents who eventually toppled and beheaded him.

Now as then, there have been few tangible signs of improvement under the western-backed regime. Despite the US pouring approximately $80bn into Afghanistan, the roads in Kabul are still more rutted than those in the smallest provincial towns of Pakistan. There is little health care; for any severe medical condition, patients still have to fly to India. A quarter of all teachers in Afghanistan are themselves illiterate. In many areas, district governance is almost non-existent: half the governors do not have an office, more than half have no electricity, and most receive only $6 a month in expenses. Civil servants lack the most basic education and skills.

This is largely because $76.5bn of the $80bn committed to the country has been spent on military and security, and most of the remaining $3.5bn on international consultants, some of whom are paid in excess of $1,000 a day, according to an Afghan government report. This, in turn, has had other negative effects. As in 1842, the presence of large numbers of well-paid foreign troops has caused the cost of food and provisions to rise, and living standards to fall. The Afghans feel they are getting poorer, not richer.

There are other similarities. Then as now, the war effort was partially privatised: it was not so much the British army as a corporation, the East India Company, that provided most of the troops who fought the war for Britain in 1842, just as today both the British and the Americans have subcontracted much of their security work to private companies. When I visited the British embassy, I found that many of the security guards at the gatehouse were not army or military police, but from Group 4 Security. The US security contracts offered to Blackwater/Xe and other private security forces under Dick Cheney's ideologically driven policy of privatising war are worth many millions of dollars.

Finally, now as then, there has been an attempt at a last show of force in order to save face before withdrawal. As happened in 1842, it has achieved little except civilian casualties and the further alienation of the Afghans. As one of the tribal elders from Jegdalek said to me: "How many times can they apologise for killing our innocent women and children and expect us to forgive them? They come, they bomb, they kill us and then they say, 'Oh, sorry, we got the wrong people.' And they keep doing that."

The British soldiers of 1842 found the same reaction in their day. In his diary of his time with the British army of retribution, which laid waste to great areas of southern Afghanistan as punishment for the massacres on the retreat from Kabul earlier in the year, the young Captain N Chamberlain reported how his troops inflicted horrible atrocities on any Afghan civilians they could find. One morning he met a wounded Afghan woman dragging herself towards a stream with a water pot. "I filled the vessel for her," he wrote, "but all she said was, 'Curses on the feringhees [foreigners]!' I continued on my way disgusted with myself, the world, above all with my cruel profession. In fact, we are nothing but licensed assassins."

However, there are some important differences between Britain's first defeat in Afghanistan and the current mess. In 1842, we were at least reinstalling a legitimate Afghan ruler and removing one who could genuinely be cast as an illegitimate usurper. Shah Shuja, the British puppet, was a former ruler of the Sadozai dynasty, from the leading Pashtun clan, and a grandson of the great Ahmed Shah Durrani, the first king of a united Afghanistan. As the traveller and pioneering archaeologist Charles Masson observed: "The Afghans had no objection to the match; they merely disliked the manner of the wooing."

This time, we have been clumsier, and NATO has helped install a former CIA asset accused by a high-ranking UN diplomat of drug abuse and of having a history of mental instability, with little to recommend him other than that he was once run out of Langley. Although Karzai is a Pashtun of the Popalzai tribe, under his watch NATO has in effect installed the Northern Alliance in Kabul and driven the country's Pashtun majority out of power.

The reality of our present Afghan entanglement is that we took sides in a complex civil war, which has been running since the 1970s, siding with the north against the south, town against country, secularism *against Islam, and the Tajiks against the Pashtuns. We have installed a government, and trained up an army, both of which in many ways have discriminated against the Pashtun majority, and whose top-down, highly centralised constitution allows for remarkably little federalism or regional representation. However much western liberals may dislike the Taliban – and they have very good reason for doing so – the truth remains that they are in many ways the authentic voice of rural Pashtun conservatism, whose views and wishes are ignored by the government in Kabul and who are still largely excluded from power. It is hardly surprising that the Pashtuns are determined to resist the regime and that the insurgency is widely supported, especially in the Pashtun heartlands of the south and east.*

Yet it is not too late to learn some lessons from the mistakes of the British in 1842. Then, British officials in Kabul continued to send out despatches of delusional optimism as the insurgents moved ever closer to Kabul, believing that there was a straightforward military solution to the problem and that if only they could recruit enough Afghans to their army, they could eventually march out, leaving that regime in place – exactly the sentiments expressed by the Defence Secretary, Liam Fox, on his visit to Afghanistan last month.

In 1842, by the time they realised they had to negotiate a political solution, their power had ebbed too far, and the only thing the insurgents were willing to negotiate was an unconditional surrender. Today, too, there is no easy military solution to Afghanistan: even if we proceed with the plan to equip an army of half a million troops (at the cost of roughly $2bn a year, when the entire revenue of the Afghan government is $1.1bn – in other words, 180 per cent of revenue), that army will never be able to guarantee security or shore up such a discredited regime. Every day, despite the military power of the US and Nato and the $25bn so far ploughed into rebuilding the Afghan army, security gets worse, and the area under government control contracts week by week.

The only answer is to negotiate a political solution while we still have enough power to do so, which in some form or other involves talking to the Taliban. This is a course that Karzai, to his credit, is keen to pursue; he made it clear that his peace jirga at the start of this month was open to any Taliban leader willing to lay down arms, and that jobs and monetary incentives would be available to former Taliban who changed their allegiance and joined the government. It is still unclear whether the new Tory government supports this course; Barack Obama certainly opposes it. In this, he is supported by the notably undiplomatic US envoy to the region, Richard Holbrooke, described by one senior British diplomat as "a bull who brings his own china shop wherever he goes".

There is something else we can still do before we pull out: leave some basic infrastructure behind, a goal we notably failed to achieve in the past nine years. Yet William Hague and Liam Fox oppose this policy – as Fox notoriously said in his 21 May interview with the Times, which infuriated his Afghan hosts: "We are not in Afghanistan for the sake of the education policy in a broken 13th-century country." The Tories could do much worse than consult their own newly elected backbencher Rory Stewart. He knows much more about Afghanistan than either Fox or Hague. As Stewart wrote shortly before he entered politics, targeted aid projects that employ Afghans can do a great deal of good, "and we should focus on meeting the Afghan government's request for more investment in agriculture, irrigation, energy and roads".

In the meantime, Obama has announced that he will begin withdrawing troops in July 2011. The start of the US withdrawal is likely to begin a rush to evacuate the other Nato forces located in pockets around the country: the Dutch have announced that they will be pulling out of Uruzgan this summer, and the Canadian and Danes won't be far behind them. Nor will the Brits, despite assurances from Hague and Fox. A recent poll showed that 72 per cent of Britons want their troops out of Afghanistan immediately, and there is only so long any government can hold out against such strong public opinion. Certainly, it is time to shed the idea that a pro-western puppet regime that excludes the Pashtuns can remain in place indefinitely. The Karzai government is crumbling before our eyes, and if we delude ourselves that this is not the case, we could yet face a replay of 1842.

George Lawrence, a veteran of that war, issued a prescient warning in the Times just before Britain blundered into the Second Anglo-Afghan War in the 1870s. "A new generation has arisen which, instead of profiting from the solemn lessons of the past, is willing and eager to embroil us in the affairs of that turbulent and unhappy country," he wrote. "Although military disasters may be avoided, an advance now, however successful in a military point of view, would not fail to turn out to be as politically useless."

William Dalrymple's latest book, "Nine Lives: in Search of the Sacred in Modern India", won the first Asia House Literary Award in May, and is newly published in paperback (Bloomsbury, £8.99). His book on the First Anglo-Afghan War is planned for release in autumn 2012.

I have had written permission from William Dalrymple to quote him through his books and to include this article in my manuscript.

I cannot wait to read his book planned for release next year. I am a fan of his writing. I hope you found the above article interesting and informative. Like all of history, it tells a story and the fact that Dalrymple actually entered such a dangerous zone is extremely courageous.

One thing is omnipresent, however, and that is the spirit of these people; the Afghanis for sure, but I also mean the people of India and Pakistan; that time or turmoil cannot repress. The Afghanis are courageous and have great fortitude. The Indians and Pakistanis are enterprising, intelligent and industrious; they aspire to success through education and hard work. To them, education is paramount. They must have it as surely as they must have oxygen to breathe. Their diligence is bound to bring them to their glory in a new age. I am ever optimistic. It is the Asian way.

Please do not be influenced to believe that all Muslims are terrorists, extremists and bad people as seems to be the norm of thinking in the West today. I know the media puts out this reportage without real details. The terrorists and extremists are truly a minority in Pakistan and even in Afghanistan, the normal people in both these two countries are more victimized by terrorism than we are in the West. The majority of the Islamic people are a wonderful race of human beings. They are generous, kind, extremely hospitable; from the rich to the very poor. They are also very respectful of other religions and beliefs, despite what the media puts out. Of course, like any other race of people, the fanatics and the trouble makers exist and it is these groups that give the whole of Islam a bad name. In Pakistan there are also many problems with existing political issues. Remember it is a fairly new country. Many said at its birth in 1947 and in its infancy that Pakistan would not last one year; never survive, but it has. I was there when it was 'born' amid bloodshed and chaos. I saw the misery, the suffering and most of all the fortitude of the people of the country perhaps that is why I feel so strongly about its concept.

It is a country of much trouble and destruction but I still feel bound to it. My children were born there and my brother, a Wing Commander in the PAF died for the country. As Diana Quick's book title states, *A Tug on the Thread*, well; I too feel that tug on the thread.

It is morning and I must get up and live in the real world – there is always another
night to dream . . .

Helen Renaux

Chapter Two

Childhood years

My dear Grandchildren

Now to give you a feeling of what it was like to live in India as a child. I can only speak for myself here. Of course I will include my immediate family.

'Hookee how, how, hooh'!

That was the sound of the jackals' call to my childish ears as I lay tucked in my bed at night. Those jackals' cries, that continued to haunt me for what seemed to be for hours and hours, were the horror of my nights. Even though, it was a normal nightly happening, the sound was eerie and made me think of someone in pain. I was not scared of them, just did not like the way they sounded. Their call disturbed my equilibrium.

I cannot remember the town I was born in, Ferozepore (now in India by the partitioning of the country) because my parents were transferred elsewhere when I was two years old, just after my brother, Derrick, was born. My mother told me that I was very excited about the new baby that was coming to our family, but as soon as I saw him, I scratched his face.

I am now writing what my mother told me. We moved to a place called, Bahawalnagar, one of the many towns where my father was stationed, because he was employed by the North Western Railway. Bahawalnagar was situated in the east/central part of the Punjab, just east of the Sutlej River. The Sutlej is the longest of the five rivers of the Punjab. These five rivers made the Punjab the most fertile plain in India. The word Punjab translated breaks down as follows: Panch (meaning five) and Ab (meaning river). However, the British renamed everything and so it became 'Punjab'.

We never seemed to stay very long in any one place when my father and my mother were young. Being a railway man he was moved from place to place; to name but a few of these towns: Sibi, Kotri, Khanewal, Nowshera, Rawalpindi, Peshawar, Cawnpore etc. Not that you would know of any of these, however, during your life time you may just hear of them or may perhaps travel there.

I could go on and on naming places that we stayed in and visited. Some of these names are now changed because of the division of the sub-continent, but some still remain the same. Some have developed into big market towns, whereas when I was there they were small towns with just a railway station, a few shops and houses and lots of 'maidans' (playing fields). The openness and vastness of the country on the whole was quite staggering, even to a native of the country. Perhaps I am looking at the vastness and space through childhood eyes.

I can remember facts from the age of three, but I won't bore you with too many of them but will recount those I think you might find interesting or amusing.

I was really little (about three or four) I remember my mother having the *dursie* (tailor) make me a pretty dress and knickers to match. I was so proud of my outfit (important to me even in those very young years; everything had to co-ordinate and match) and so I decided to show it to my father who was sitting in the garden, entertaining friends. I proudly displayed my dress, did a twirl and then lifted the skirt with both hands to show the knickers to match.

The reason this sticks in my mind is because instead of getting my father's approval and admiration, he told me off and said that nice girls did not display their knickers in front of guests. I was gutted and ran into the house.

Another memory I have when I was about five years old, was being taken by train to Agra to see various Mughal buildings with the Taj being the highlight. I remember the journey, but did not absorb much else. I saw the Taj, but I was too young to appreciate anything. My brother, Derrick, who was too young to be my playmate, was no company for me. All I wanted to do was to expend energy. I wish now I had listened and looked. I loved a train journey to any where. It was the travelling that was the enjoyment for me. It still is today. I love the changing panorama of a journey, whether by air, sea, rail or road.

I am inserting an article I wrote some time back for an Indian Railway magazine. It is to give you a feeling and idea of the opulence of train travel in the days of the Raj and the prestige of the great Frontier Mail – the train my Dad, your great grandfather, was very proud to drive.

As a child I did a great deal of railway travel in India and this article will give you an insight into a part of my life that I loved.

Memoirs of train journeys during the Raj
By Helen Renaux

THE FRONTIER MAIL, which ran from Peshawar in the North West Frontier Province to Bombay (now Mumbai) in Central Provinces, was the first luxurious, prestigious and fastest train in the Indian Subcontinent. During the Raj years it was partly used for carrying troops; unloading cargo and for troops boarding ships to and from the UK and of course for the speedy transfer of mail. The soldiers travelled on third and second class tickets; the officers and civilian senior railway personnel travelled First Class. It was a luxury passenger train with a red mail coach attached. The train was then pulled by the enormous steam engines of the day.

A saloon car on the GIP Railway.

Below Frontier Mail at a station.

Frontier Mail leaving a railway station near Bombay (now Mumbai).

The Frontier Mail made its debut in 1928 and received the accolade in 1930, by The Times of London, to be named as the fastest train in the British Empire. My father was a senior driver of this very train during the years of 1930 to 1937! He was known by his colleagues as 'Speed King Percy' because he held the record of driving his train in the fastest time and, as far as I know, his record was never beaten in his life time. He died at the age of 48 of pneumonia; (a comparatively young man). Pneumonia was a deadly disease in those years before antibiotics. He loved speed in other ways too. He owned the fastest motor bike of the time and the fastest racing car. He was a scholar and a speed freak.

In 1934 the Frontier Mail was also the first train in the Indian Peninsula to have an Air Conditioned compartment, used mainly by the elite passengers of the British Raj.

I remember travelling in the Frontier Mail as a child. We moved from place to place, and so we had our own bogey (carriage) – one bogey for our goods and furniture and a six berth carriage for the family. My Dad did not always drive the engine during these journeys but when he was the driver he joined us for a meal at long waiting stops.

We travelled in style. Our compartments had leather (or look alike—I am not quite sure) berths which had back rests in upholstered buttoned down material similar to the seats one sat on. These back rests could be folded down if one wanted to use the berth as a bed or kept upright in the day as a couch. The upper berths were well padded beds but could be locked upright during the day to give more space. The middle top berth stayed in situ because the centre berth was clear and could be used as a couch or just something to lounge on. Each compartment had its own WC and wash basin with running water. The wash basin was made of stainless steel and folded up when not in use to give one more space in the small, compact room. As far as I remember the toilet seat too was made of stainless steel.

Knowing the luxury used in the days of the Raj, the material of the berths was probably made of real leather. The train was not a walk-through train like the trains in UK. The bogies were all separate carriages. There was an emergency pull chain, but if one used it casually, there was a large fine, so we children were warned never to pull the chain.

Before Air Conditioning was installed we had electric fans. I think there were six in each six berth carriage. The windows had two kinds of shutters; one mesh to stop insects but allow air through. This could be opened or closed at will. The other one was made of polished slatted wood. The shutters were maneuverable. The slats could be opened or shut to darken the carriage from the heat of the sun. There were locks on the door and the windows for safety on the journey and at stops during the night. The windows also had pull down blinds – again to cut out glare and heat.

In later years the windows were made of large sheets of tinted glass which cut out glare and was suitable for air conditioning. This was eventually installed in all first class carriages in about the late 1950's and 1960's.

Every driver travelled with his batman (assistant). That is the name my father used for his helper, because my father's family was all military men. The assistant did odd chores of running about on platforms when the train was stationery, getting anything that was needed and seeing to the welfare of the family in general.

We were served with Spencer's food by liveried bearers (waiters). The food was served on silver trays, with silver cutlery and bone china Spencer logo crockery! The plates and tea services were white with a green and a gold stripe around the boarder and the Spencer logo on each piece of crockery. The meals were strategically ordered at one station. The waiters would board with their menus at one of the stations. We would order from an a la carte menu. They then sent the order to the next station by whatever communication was used in those days and we would be served the food choices at the following station; the used trays and crockery being cleared at yet another station. The timings of the stops were coincided with meal times as the journeys were long, sometimes running into 48 hours depending on one's destination.

In later years the Frontier Mail had its own restaurant car or dining car.

The Frontier Mail ran like clock work – arriving at each station on time. Of course there were the usual hold ups of signal failure, cattle crossing the tracks at villages etc. But the main objective was to arrive at all the main stations on time. This is where my father was known for making up lost time with speed! The trains were never late.

Sleeping on trains was a joy to me and to most children – perhaps adults too. I loved the rhythm of the wheels on the track, the chug of the steam locomotives and the rocking motion of the train. It was like a sedative and we kids slept well.

Since I was 11 years old when my father died, I have a good recall of these exciting and memorable journeys. We children loved the noise, the hustle and bustle of the various platforms where the train stopped; the calling of wares 'gharam gharam chai' (hot, hot tea) is one I remember well and many other sellers of sweet meats and delicacies wandered the length of the platforms calling out their wares which we were not allowed to eat, much to our disappointment!

We loved our Spencer meals though as they were restaurant class. There were steaks, grills, casseroles, stews, delicious fish and some Indian dishes too to select from.

Yes, my childhood and the North Western Railway are truly tied up with golden memories.

As an adult I had the privilege of travelling on the famous Deccan Queen from Bombay to Poona (now Mumbai to Pune). I was about 19 years old in actuality but 21 according to the Royal Air Force. I had bluffed my age to join the WACS and was seconded to the RAF. I was on my way to Poona/Lonavla for training to be an officer. There were twenty five of us on the trip; 20 men and about 5 women. We travelled First class in air conditioned carriages. As it was a moderately short journey by Indian standards, there were no berths, but very plush seating accommodation. It was a bit similar to the saloon picture above.

The train travelled through the Western Ghats – sometimes through rugged hills and at other times, through lush greenery. The railway track was built through and on the hills; at times one could look out of the window and see the edge of a deep precipice and nothing else because the track ran extremely close to the ledge. It was a hair-raising experience. The scenery however was spectacular. We went through many tunnels.

The first leg of this particular journey must have been on the Frontier Mail, because we travelled from

33

Lahore to Bombay and that was the main train that did that journey. It was a sociable journey with plenty of Gin and Tonics, Nimbu panis and other alcoholic and non-alcoholic cocktails. We were young officer cadets having a wonderful time.

The British did a remarkable job building these Indian Railways and they run today without the steam locomotives one has to admit; and they run on time!

My brother Mervyn was born in Ludhiana but I do not remember this place much, nor my brother being a baby. Perhaps I was with my grandparents in Karachi at the time. He was five years junior to me. I do remember one thing about Mervyn as a small child. He was five and my sister three when my father died and they were sent to my boarding school in Murree as a special admission because my mother could not look after them for a short while. They were being cared for in the nursery in my school. Mervyn was always cheeky and he was cheeky to me. We had a quarrel and he physically attacked me. I lifted a small chair to defend myself and he rushed into me and got a cut on his head by the chair. I adored him and my horror at having done this to my little brother upset me so much that I started crying and saying how sorry I was. Mervyn just kept saying it was nothing and was consoling me instead. That is the kind of person he was even as a little babe of five.

He was a solid little fellow with a beautiful face. My sister was like a doll for me to play with. She had light hair and blue/green eyes. I loved having my sibling with me in school. Mervyn's stay was short and he was taken back home in a couple of months. Gwen stayed on for a short time longer, but then she too went back home as soon as Mum was better.

To continue in chronological order with my story, by now we had moved to Rawalpindi, where my sister was born.

As the years moved on and we grew a little, my sister and I were pet lovers and my brothers, who had air guns, shot everything in sight that was wild and little such as sparrows, squirrels and anything that moved. I hated them for this and often hid their guns, which incurred many a quarrel. My sister was little and just tagged along and did whatever I told her.

I used to collect baby sparrows that fell out of their nests, perhaps because my brothers shot their parents. I nursed them from little meat balls and taught them how to fly by throwing them into the air. They used to walk on their little legs behind me all the time and I was scared they would get trodden on. Most of my sparrows learned to fly and some never returned. One little fellow would not fly and walked behind me all the time. Somehow I must have gone wrong with this one because he never understood that he was a bird.

I remember that we went to a fair close by and without my knowledge my little sparrow was walking behind me, and yes, the inevitable happened—he was crushed and my heart was broken. We had a funeral when we came home which was solemn, sad and very tearful. Even my brothers were sad.

I also kept baby squirrels (grey chipmunks). They were a delight and gave many hours of fun. They too were nursed from little meat balls and I fed them with cotton wool sticks. They grew fat and beautiful, but I never kept them caged. They were free to roam and they did. Some went back to a wild state but some insisted on following me everywhere. While peddling my bicycle at high speed along the pathway from our home, I would see one of my squirrels in the field trying to keep up with me. They would eventually run up a tree and watch me as I rode on to the main road.

Throughout my life I had pets, dogs, cats, lambs and even a donkey that was called 'Rastas', but this is way out of chronological order and I will come back to Rastas later.

Some of you have visited Mumbai, but that might not help you to realise or visualise the vastness of India. The Punjab plains where we spent most of our childhood were something else. I do not think any of you have visited the really Northern areas of Pakistan where the real beauty of the subcontinent is seen in all its grandeur. However my siblings and I lived there with very happy memories.

As children we were like any other Anglo Indian railway family. We lived in a big brick house with many rooms, high ceilings with skylight windows under the ceilings, to let out rising heat. These skylights had long cords that enabled opening and closing. Every room was fitted with large electric fans, and there was a veranda that encircled the entire house, with arches where *chiks* (thick bamboo cane blinds) were hung. These kept the house cool in the heat of the day. The servants rolled them up in the evenings when the sun was low on the horizon.

As soon as the sun's heat began to pall the *Mali* (gardener) would water the garden and the patio area where a table and chairs were set out for the evening. Besides the table and chairs there were *morahs* (cane chairs) and recliner chairs which were made of polished wood; cross work cane seats and backs, for coolness; with folding and extending armrests so one could put one's feet up if one felt the need to. All this furniture was moved out of the veranda and into the garden in the evening for before dinner drinks and entertaining and at night returned to the veranda when we retired. Sometimes on hot nights, the servants laid the dining table out doors and we ate out, with pedestal fans keeping insects away from the food and keeping us cool.

When our parents and friends socialised in the garden, the *Bearer* or *kitmagar* (a sort of over bearer) would serve the famous *nimbu pani* ('nimbu' is lime and 'pani' is water) in tall slim glasses with ice cubes tinkling and decorative slices of lime which added a touch of extra flavour and colour. This drink is still a great favourite in India and Pakistan because it is cooling and thirst quenching. However, this was followed by canapés and John Colin's and Tom Colin's cocktails, for the adults. We children soon had to say goodnight and go to bed to read and sleep after the jackals had had their howling session.

I will never forget the smell that exuded from the earth after the evening watering. It was a very special smell of the heat rising out of the dampened earth. It was an earthy scent yet particularly heady.

Nor will I forget that I loved the smell of petrol as I sat on my Dad's motorbike, opened the tank and sniffed the petrol in perfect innocence but it was 'heady' and enjoyable. I did it once or twice until I was seen and my Dad was told. Needless to add, I never did it again! I loved his motor bike and often sat on it. The petrol business was curiosity because I undid the screw top to the petrol tank just to sniff it. The effect was more than I expected! I was eight years old.

Our servants (our best friends really) consisted of a cook, a *bearer a kitmagar*, a cleaner, a *Mather (*who cleaned the bathrooms) an *ayah*, a *Mali (*the gardener) and a couple of others who helped. We adored our servants. Each house had servants' quarters, quite apart from the house, as was the kitchen. The grounds of the houses were extensive and we had plenty of room to play.

We children were not allowed to visit the servants' houses, but that was one of our greatest pleasures and we did visit them and were welcomed.

'*Bheto, Baba'* (sit children or child) and they fed us their meagre food of dhal and chapattis, sometimes with a little vegetable.

They all sat together around an *inghiti* (like a little barbecue) on which everything was cooked. Some servants cooked on a *chula,* clay plastered oven with a hole on top for wood or charcoal and an oven underneath to keep things hot. These primitive clay cookers were quite ingenious. The servants ground their spices on a flat stone and rounded stone; both the base stone and the rounded grinding stone were extremely heavy (much better that a pestle and mortar). The rounded stone was held by both hands and was moved back and forth to grind the spices and a splash of water was added frequently to make the spices into a paste.

After making dough out of chapatti flour, they made round balls of flour, flattened them with their finger tips then flicked them between the palms until they were round and very fine and then cooked on a *tawa* (a heavy flat pan) similar to a pancake griddle pan. The chapattis were then transferred to a *thali*, a large metal flat dish and covered with a cloth to keep them warm. Nothing in the world tasted so good to us as that simple food; perhaps because it was forbidden that this food was much appreciated.

Our parents were busy doing other things and we children had a lot of freedom to wander in the *maidans* (country grounds) near by, visit our friends and generally do as we pleased, outdoors of course. Indoors, we had to behave. Table manners were strictly adhered to. We were taught etiquette in most things from a very young age. Because our lives were so free (apart from school) I now realise how precious that freedom, space, safety and security was to us and how lucky we were to have experienced it. Our servants were ever watchful over us and our parents trusted them.

As we grew a bit older we had bikes and were able to go even further afield, but our parents did have a say in where and when we used our bikes.

Gwen and I rode hill ponies as both of us loved riding. I have always loved horses and seem to have an affinity with them. I rode a horse in Murree that was known to be difficult to ride because of its temperament. His name was Black Prince and he was black and shiny. I rode him against all advice and he bolted on a narrow and dangerous mountain path. I gave him a fairly loose rein and let him run. After a great deal of hair raising scares on my part he eventually calmed down and trotted gingerly back to base, to the surprise of his *syce* (groom) who, I am sure, expected to see horse but no rider! I always rode Black Prince when I got the opportunity and he never misbehaved with me again.

Chapter Three

Teenage Years

Hello again my darling grandchildren

Teenage years were the same as any other teenager years of more recent times. We revolted, we were going to change the world and knew the answer to everything – or thought we did. I was flippant even in those days when it was not really the norm to be rude; to answer back. However, it was not as bad as today, because most of the year we were in boarding school so our parents had a break for nine months of the year! Besides when we were home we had space to express ourselves. There was so much to do; whether it was mischief, like scrumping or otherwise, we were always on the go and our bikes were our mode of transport.

We had no portable equipment like iPods or mobiles and no television. The outdoors was our playground. Our music came from radios that remained indoors. We did have voices and we sang a lot.

We travelled in gangs, similar to today, and I had many friends. We kept up (through radio) with the music of our era, jazz, jive, jitterbug and rock 'n roll. We had our tea dances in the various venues set out for teenagers. Those dances were as energetic as the dances of today. Perhaps street dancing today has one up on us in those days but only just a bit. We did not spin on our heads though we were very athletic in the moves.

My mother and all of us; by now the family had increased—three boys and two girls lived in a town called Meerut. Meerut was a military town and my third brother, Raymond, was a baby and I enjoyed looking after him. He had blue eyes and light hair. He still has the most beautiful blue eyes today and looks like his Dad, Walter, my step father. His blue eyes are startling in a ruddy skinned complexion, and even to this day he is considered good looking. From my gorgeous looking little brother back to geography and humanity.

Meerut, the city we were in, is located to the north-east of New Delhi, in the state of Uttar Pradesh. The Meerut district has a population of approximately 2.5 million. However, the city itself has a little over 1 million inhabitants. Delhi is about 70 kilometers away from Meerut. These statistics are present day. When we lived there the population figures must have been much lower but my research has not been able to locate this figure.

In Meerut, I was fourteen and I had my first boyfriend, whose name was Carlton Chase. I say 'boyfriend' but all we did was talk and walk out together and play games that were totally innocent and fun. He was hunky and I remember him well. We ate meals in each others houses. We were kids, not like the young teens of today who hardly seem to have a childhood at all. Of course there was the odd kiss goodnight, which was fun too.

From Meerut we moved to Lucknow. We lived in a huge house and there were vast areas within our own grounds for us to play. It was a famous military base which was the reason for my step Dad's posting there. Lucknow is also a historic city and I will tell you a bit about it.

The city of Lucknow was large and had, and still has a popular university. However, the city is caught in a time warp. It exists in an in-between land of the past and the present, looking back constantly to the memories of a colonial-Nawabi (Princely State). There is at the same time a sense of pride at the thought of being, after Delhi, the most important center of power in free India. Politics has been Lucknow's history but culture has been its main forte.

In the annals of Indian history, Lucknow formed a link between tradition and modernity, the decline of the Mughals and the rise of the British. The timing of its rise, however, cut short Lucknow's cultural affluence. The land of etiquette and manners of the people received a serious jolt with the siege of the British Residency during the great revolt by the Indians against the British in 1857. Eager for revenge, the British chose the last Nawab, (Prince) Wajid Ali Shah, as a suitable scapegoat. Awadh (a state) was annexed on the pretext of administrative failure and the Nawab was packed off to Calcutta with a pension. This was a fate similar for most of the Nawabs or Princes of the various states. They were dominated by British rule and had little choice but to accept whatever the British offered and to submit their territories and their wealth. Some were allowed to live in their palaces but without authority or control. On the face of things if they were allowed control it was well and truly supervised by the British rule; the British Resident of each state. This was the sad fate of the Princes of India.

Most of the Princely States were captured and the rich princes were soon 'deprived' of their wealth. This did not happen immediately. The princes held hunting parties for the British Resident and officers, who loved to shoot the beautiful Indian tigers. This was a sort of bribe that was offered to the British to enable the rajas (princes) to keep their states from being usurped. There are many pictures available in the libraries showing a glorious tiger lying dead with a British foot resting on it, posing for a picture. This was and still is a repellant sight to me and many others who loved the tigers of India. Perhaps not face to face, but just to know they existed in the jungle. The princes provided the elephants for the hunters to ride in a *howdah* (a sort of enclosed contraption) on the back of the elephant. Some principals of the British colonial reign had an elephant or two of their own as pets for their children and themselves, but most depended on the generosity of the Princes. I want to mention this because it is part of the history of India and the breaking up of the princely states with the gradual destruction and demise of the beautiful beasts that roamed in the open forests and jungles of India.

Because we lived in a sprawling house in Lucknow with extensive grounds we were not allowed to wander out in the city much. We were for most of the year in our hill schools and came home for the holidays in the winter months, from the last week of November to mid-March.

From Lucknow, my Dad was posted to Sialkot, where my brother Ralph was born. Dad was away in the Middle East with General Montgomery's army. We lived in a sprawling house and we had lots of animals. Dad left home for Cairo and fought in the war with General Montgomery; left a quiet and innocent man and came back worldly wise and so very different. I for one did not like the way he changed. I waited for a chance to leave home.

Whilst living in Sialkot, I purchased a baby donkey from a camel caravan, travelling down the road past our house. I spotted this tiny little donkey. If you have ever seen a baby donkey you will realise why I was besotted. They are the cutest little creatures with soft eyes and lovely faces. I accosted a large man leading a camel; a Pathan, and asked him if he wanted to sell the little donkey. He looked at me with disdain, vaguely surprised that a young girl had the effrontery to speak to him a grown man in that manner. I waved a note at him, not quite sure what denomination it was, but his eyes lit up and we exchanged money for donkey. I named my donkey 'Rastas' and loved him dearly. Rastas was a very spoiled donkey, I allowed him indoors and he was cuddled by me and my siblings. We had two dogs, a lamb, a cat, a minor bird who mimicked everyone and Rastas. Rastas was treated the same as our house pets. Let me add that all this nonsense of allowing him indoors went on whilst my Mother was at work as a senior nurse in the British Military Hospital. When she was home, the animals stayed outdoors.

One day about dinner time Rastas walked into the dining room, grabbed the table cloth with his teeth and walked out, pulling the fully laid dining table with cloth, crockery, cutlery, bread baskets and glasses, jugs of water and everything on it with him. When Mum came home she was very angry; the *bearer* (waiter) stood with his hand clapped to his mouth in horror. Mum said Rastas had to go the next day and that was that. He had already chewed the clothes from the washing line and was whacked by the *dhobi* (washer man), he had wandered into the kitchen and upset the cook, he got his head stuck into the loop of a wicker basket full of pans and bolted, the noise frightening him and he galloped further, on to the road, into a neighbour's garden with me giving chase until I managed to catch him and calm him down.

Rastas was no longer a baby donkey – he was growing fast but was still a spoiled pet. I knew I had to think up something or my Rastas would be given away to work for his living. We children thought furiously and fast about how we could save Rastas. We decided we would train him to carry Ralph, who was the baby at the time, on his back.

Secretly, Mum loved Rastas too and so with a lot of persuasion and cajoling on our part, with me as the instigator, she finally capitulated and we all had to train Rastas with a saddle, stirrups and bridal. He kicked, he jumped and wiggled to try to dislodge this foreign thing on his back, but we knew he had to get used to it or else he was out. He eventually did get used to the harness and saddle seat – this makes it sound easy – it was not. It was hard work to get a spoiled pet to realise he was really a beast of burden. Poor Rastas!

Eventually we put weights in the saddle and made him walk and he did so with dignity and we thought it was time to try to put Ralph in the saddle. Mum was at work, Dad was abroad and I was in charge. I put Ralph in the saddle, which had a secure little seat and he was locked in. My heart was thumping. What if he bolted with Ralph, I would have been . . . what? I dare not think. Rastas didn't budge. I tentatively took the bridal rein and walked him around. It was magic. Rastas was giving Ralph a ride. Ralph loved it and so did we and by the look of things, Rastas felt important because of all the love he was getting from us. The end of the story is that Rastas stayed on and took Ralph for many a walk around our extensive grounds. He was sadly given to a friend with a baby where he continued with his services because we had to move again and we were not allowed to take Rastas on the train with us.

I left home at the age of seventeen and joined the Air Force during the Second World War telling them I was nineteen, the qualifying age to join. My Dad was now stationed in Lahore. It was quite near the end of the war, but I wanted to be free and stay with other girls in military accommodation. My boss at the RAF base and I fell in love or so I thought at the time. After a hectic courtship we became engaged and my parents thought he was wonderful, so did I. He was very good looking. The 'love' on my side was a bit shallow I think, because when I had a letter from his parents in England discouraging me by saying that if he and I got married, I would not be accepted in his country (England) and that our children, if we had any, would be considered outcasts. It was an awful letter and I broke off the engagement immediately and the poor man suffered for his parents' prejudice. He was very upset and kept visiting my home, but I was always out with someone else. My Dad consoled him and so did my Mum but I had lost all interest in him by this time.

How glad I am today that this love affair (if that's what it was; I was too young to know) ended. I would not have my treasured children and none of you either. What a tragedy that would have been!

I could tell you a lot about my young years and all the fun I had, but it is not the purpose of this manuscript. It is not my autobiography, but enlightenment for you to know about your ancestors and about the country where all our roots lie.

It is man that can make the Way great, and not the Way that can makes man great.

Confucius

Chapter Four

Noel and Norma

My dear Grandchildren

I have to say a little about your granddad, Noel and me here, the parents of your parents.

I didn't want marriage – life was too full for me. I was busy having fun with many friends both male and female and I certainly did not want children. However, your Granddad Noel had other ideas and was a very persistent suitor. We met officially at a tea dance (or jam session) as we called them, which were common in those days. They were held in the afternoon in big hotels or night clubs (about 5 pm) with a live band and dancing and lots of alcohol or tea if you preferred. My friend introduced us because she was married to Noel's brother and she knew I loved dancing. When she said he was the best dancer, I was ready to meet him. I always loved to dance. It was customary in those days of good manners and etiquette that the boy approached a girl and asked her to dance. I pretended not to look, but I did watch surreptitiously as he swaggered across the floor and approached me.

'Hi, want to dance?' I expected something more like, 'May I have the pleasure of this dance.' Oh well I danced and he was heaven to dance with. When the tea dance was over about 10pm, we went off together to have dinner in one of the many night clubs in Lahore, then danced the night away till the early dawn.

That was the start of a ten year romance that included every emotion that existed within it. Noel, I learned later had seen me riding my bike past his house for a long time and had every intention of making my acquaintance.

Well the night was great and I discovered he was in demand by other girls—always a lady's man! As time went on we were together a lot, and even though I was not ready for any commitment he would not take no for an answer, besides he demolished every other man who had any interest in me (and there were many) or even innocents who just looked at me. He was a terror in that respect – a fighter—who wanted me for himself, but apart from this he was the most affable, charming and popular person you could meet. He was popular with both women and men. His had personality with a wonderfully dry, cryptic sense of humour, the best dancer, tough and masculine and hence popular with the females. Because he was so tough he was therefore respected by men.

My brother Derrick and Neville Hine were his best friends and could tell you a tale or two about him. They were very close.

In brief I married him for two reasons – first I loved him more than any other man, because I respected him for his love, his loyalty and his sheer power of personality. The other reason I married him was because he would not allow another man near me for any length of time – his persistent and constant pursuit wore me down. He was a boxer who was selected for the world Olympics, but broke his arm just before the time. Basically my parents disapproved of Noel because of his boxing, hell raising and drinking but to me he was a real fun person to be with.

I tried meeting others to please or pacify my parents and also to try to defeat this forceful man who was pursuing me with such persistent intent. I got engaged six times – all to no avail. He got rid of all the fiancées, systematically, in his own dogmatic way. Some stood up to him and tried to fight for their rights, but he conquered eventually. All this took part over a period of ten years. He just would not give me up. How could I not be impressed? There is so much more I could write about him – it would fill this document and leave room for nothing else. Suffice to say that he was an amazing man, this father of my children. We had a tumultuous and exciting life together but never, ever boring.

At the end of our ten year courtship, what really woke me up was to see him at a New Year's Eve ball with a very pretty woman. I went with my latest and last fiancé, who was tall, blue-eyed and very good looking with a professional position in work and totally approved of by my parents.

Noel and his lady friend had a table in this very plush hall, complete with crystal chandeliers, a sprung dance floor and a forty piece orchestra. There was a balcony running all round the hall. Noel was watching us and I was aware of it; nervous at what he would do. He invited Peter (fiancé at the time) and me to join them as we did not have a table. Everything went well and I was beginning to relax, though I did not like Noel being with this other girl. However, when they played the midnight dance, Noel ignored his date, grabbed my hand without saying a word. I had no option but to acquiesce and we danced the 'midnight ball' dance together. This dance said a lot; one danced the midnight dance at the ball with one's true love. The other two in our party were left to themselves. Immediately the dance was over, he returned to the table; left me in the middle of the floor; collected my bag, saying nothing to our companions and then escorted me to the cloak room, ordered our coats and we left. He proposed for the hundredth time on the way home and I eventually said 'yes'. I was not about to take any more chances!

I woke my sister Gwen and told her the news. She was ecstatic, as she always loved Noel and felt he was meant for me.

Eventually we were married in St Anthony's Church, Empress Road, Lahore on the 20th June 1954, with Derrick giving me away, Mervyn in attendance as our witness, Gwen as one of my bridesmaids and Jeanne (Lesley Anne's Mother) the other, and the two little flower girls, Nanette and Janette Green. My parents did not attend my wedding, but Noel's parents did. It was a happy yet sad day for me, because my Mum was not there. It was also the hottest day of the year. I will never forget how hot it was – 100°F.

We had a lovely reception in the Catholic Social Club hall near to the Cathedral. The sad thing was our photographer's camera had a fault which he discovered later. There were no official photographs – all we had were snapshots taken by a few friends.

One little incident I would like to mention is while I was getting dressed for my wedding in Jeanne's mother's house, I received a note written on the back of a cigarette pack from Noel. He was helping to decorate the Hall for the reception. On this bit of card was scribbled the words, 'To the world you are only one, to me you are the world.' These same words, slightly adjusted were written on our (my children's and mine) wreath when he died, 'To the world you were only one, to us you were the world'.

After we were married—, I remember Noel and I having our fortune1 s read by a local fortune teller. He told me I would have four children (at the time I was sure he was talking rubbish – it was not in my plans to have any). Noel was told that he would travel abroad and work in a large desert. He also told Noel that he would travel to distant lands and would live to the age of 52. Noel did travel to distant lands. Timbuktu, Mali for one amongst many, and died when he was 51 in Khartoum, Sudan.

We giggled over it at the time and went our way, never knowing how true the prophecy was going to be.

Three of my children, Roger, Diane and Caryl were baptized in the Sacred Heart Cathedral in Lahore. Lorraine who was baptized in St Lawrence Church, Cincinnatus Town, Karachi.

The Lahore Cathedral

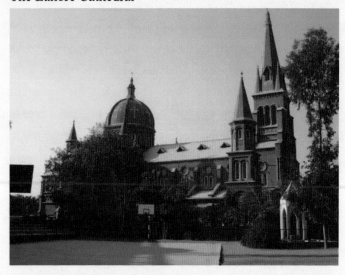

With this heritage of strong willed grandparents, perhaps now you realise why we are all part of a powerful, confident, fun loving, arrogant (if you like) family – blame it on your grandparents on one side of the family at least – both Noel and I were strong, forceful personalities. Perhaps the other side of your parents/grandparents balanced you out a bit.

Like an exploding star the death of colonization in India came suddenly, bringing in its wake violence and bloodletting

Chapter Five

The Partition of the Subcontinent

My dearest Grandchildren

This is a subject that I have put to the back of my mind; into my subconscious. I am bringing it to mind now, with pain and dread as it is a time that I really want to forget. It was a horrendous experience of terror and dread and not something I enjoy writing about. This manuscript however would not be a true history if I left out such an historical event as the dividing of a mighty subcontinent.

I will mention only a couple of incidents that involved me personally, but what affected both Indians and Muslims crossing over to the country of their choice was far more tragic and full of horror, bloodshed and mass murder. It seemed to be a time of total madness; friends turning against friends; neighbours, who had lived together in harmony, suddenly began to kill each other. It was like sitting on a time bomb.

To open this autobiographical narrative I am about to write, it is essential to first give a brief backdrop to the political and historical event which was the reason for the incident.

The partition of British India in 1947 created the two independent countries of India and Pakistan. What followed the partition was deemed the cruelest and bloodiest migration in history. Religious fury, which had been dormant for many years, suddenly erupted into violence, and hostility was unleashed. This caused the deaths of approximately two million Hindus, Muslims and Sikhs. It is estimated 75,000 women were raped in both countries and that twelve to fifteen million people were transferred across the borders. I have read of many diversifications of these figures so what I quote here is the most recent I have read. The trauma incurred between these two newly formed countries during this time was profound. It would seem that everyone had gone entirely mad.

Physical killings, bloodletting, burning of buildings, refugees, disease and general mob disturbance was rampant throughout both countries; Hindus and Sikhs massacring Muslims and visa versa.

The main reason for unrest was the British Government's decision, after much wrangling between the two main parties concerned about who should get what, the British representative, Sir Cyril Radcliffe was instructed to go ahead and he eventually drew the dividing line between the two countries of Pakistan and India and partitioned the provinces. Punjab being just one area for example; an extremely fertile and rich business area; was divided into part India and part Pakistan. In drawing the border lines for the Punjab, the British action caused one of the bloodiest feuds in history. Feelings of antagonism between Muslims, Hindus and Sikhs were strong in this newly divided area of the Punjab.

It all erupted suddenly. Where there had been peace and harmony; where the various religious groups lived together quite happily, suddenly, from the day of partition of the Punjab, feelings of antagonism became rampant and friends and neighbours began killing each other because their businesses and properties were affected on both sides of the border line of the Punjab. Basic livelihood was lost on either side and tempers became frayed and sensitive, making the situation an ugly one. Hindus fled Lahore, leaving their luxury homes with unfinished meals still on the table.

Apart from the Hindu business men, there were two fighting cultures who had occupied the Punjab in perfect harmony, the Sikhs, known as the lions of the Punjab and the Muslims, who have always been well equipped in the art of war since the days of the Moghul Dynasty. Once partition was granted, they became instant enemies. Below is one story that our family was personally involved in. There were many others, but the one below will give you a good idea of how tense and traumatic the position was for anyone living near the borders.

The story below is written in the first person and present tense to give you a feel of being witness to the event. It was written some years ago.

Hostages

Our family, a neutral family, neither Sikh nor Muslim nor Hindu, but British Christian, was caught in the middle of this turmoil. My father having retired from the British Army had opted for residence in Pakistan because we already lived in Lahore long before partition took place. We loved the city and wanted to continue to live there.

Lahore is a cultural and beautiful city, known as the Garden City. There are many art museums, large, shady green parks and beautiful gardens and it is home to the famous Lahore Fort, going back to the days of the early Mughal Emperors, and Shalimar Gardens, also built in the days of the Moghuls. Lahore, apart from its ancient history, is a well known education centre, with exclusive private schools and universities.

Within this hostile milieu was our house. A large house with extensive grounds but we are situated in a vulnerable area – a few miles from the Indian border line, which was drawn between Amritsar and Lahore.

It is a beautiful day, with sunlight flooding the dining room floor, the dust particles dancing in the shimmering sunbeams streaking through the window panes. The scent of flowers comes wafting into the house through the open windows, flowers creatively displayed in a fusion of colours that the gardener has crafted with his expertise. There are rose beds, with blooms in various shades, canna lilies in all their vivid hues, sweet-scented jasmine creepers, marigolds as large as breakfast teacups and many other tropical flower beds bordering the green lawns. One could say it is a perfect day of peace and beauty.

I am giving the cook instructions for the menu of the day, as my parents are at work. I am twenty two years of age. My fifteen year old sister is taking care of our two younger brothers who are playing on the see-saw in the garden, when suddenly there are gunshots, seemingly coming from our grounds. People are screaming and shouting.

I run out and see my siblings staring in horror at a decapitated man lying within our grounds. I quickly take them indoors to what I think is comparative safety, when suddenly a Sikh soldier enters our house with a gun in his hand. He is armed with a rifle, the revolver which he has recently fired and a sword most Sikhs carry which he had used to decapitate the Muslim.

He is a tall man with regal bearing, in army uniform. He has large brown eyes with his long hair hidden within the folds of his khaki turban. He is breathless and apprehensive.

He puts his weapons on the dining table and rushes to lock all the doors and windows. He picks up the rifle and keeps it pointed and ready. He looks at me and says, 'Do you know anything about guns?'

'Yes' – I had been trained in the Air Force during the war. I was very young but I remember my armoury lessons.

'Would you be able to reload my revolver?' and he throws a bullet belt towards me. Even though he must be afraid he shows no sign of it and is very polite. I fill the cylinders and shut the gun, putting the safety catch on. He watches me as I work and gives me a smile of approval.

My sister has an arm round each of my brothers, cuddling them. They are silent and I like to think my lack of fear has a slight calming effect on them.

The atmosphere is tense, however, with none of us knowing what the outcome of this incident will be.

'Stay together' he instructs us not unkindly, but firmly.

'Don't go near the windows or doors and don't be afraid. I am not going to harm you. I need to stay here awhile.'

This comforts me a bit, because I believe his words to be honest.

He is trembling and looks wildly about, but he does not instill fear in me. My siblings, however, are still slightly fearful and I try to pacify them. Something in the man's demeanour and manner assures me that he will not hurt us.

'What I did was wrong, but when one sees an old man, a Sikh, a harmless professor, a civilian massacred before one's eyes, one reacts without thinking. I saw the man who did it and I took revenge though revenge is not mine to take; it is wrong and I will have to pay.' It would seem he believes that he needs to give me an explanation for his deed and for holding us as hostages.

Within minutes our grounds are filled with angry, vengeful Muslims. It seems to us like hundreds, but the count is not important, it is the menacing anger of the crowd that terrifies us and terrifies the murderer in our home. As the crowd gathers in towards our home, the Sikh calls out in Urdu from behind a door—a language I understand.

'Go back. I have four children in here as captives. If you advance another step, I will kill them all.'

The crowd moves backwards away from the house.

This tall, handsome man with his soft brown eyes does not seem to me to be a brutal murderer despite the crime he has just committed. Perhaps that is why I do not fear him even though I fear the crowd. He glances at me and smiles as if reading my thoughts.

The police arrive; speak to the crowd through a megaphone warning them to be careful because of the children in the house. They tell the crowd that they have sent for the Army who will take the Sikh soldier away and he will be punished by the Army.

'Don't be afraid, I will not hurt you or your sister or brothers. I will wait for the army and will give myself up. I am sorry I have frightened you all, but there was no escape for me. They would have killed me out in the street.'

'Will the Army kill you?' I feel I need to know.

'I am not sure, but I will be punished for taking the law into my own hands. I do not think I had an option in entering your home, it was for self preservation but I did have an option about killing a man nonetheless. Our religion does not permit us to kill except in war.'

The wait seems interminable. We are tired and the boys need food and so do we but the servants cannot come in as the kitchen is located outside of the main house and I am too afraid to let my siblings out of my sight.

Suddenly there is the sound of army trucks rumbling into our driveway. Three, three-ton trucks full of soldiers. The soldiers, fully armed, stand between the house and the crowd and order the crowd to disperse.

The soldiers approach our front door and instruct our captor to open up. They take him away. He turns and gives us a wistful smile. He did not hurt us.

Just writing about it and thinking back is upsetting so I had better stop this part of my experience.

I will tell you, however, of one experience that Noel and I witnessed. We had heard that there was a train arriving with refugees from India to Lahore Cantonment, so we decided that we would go and see the train come in. It was Noel's idea and we were young and thought it would be exciting. When one is young everything is an adventure. We cycled to the station. Exciting? It was horrendous! The train arrived but no one alighted from it. People were milling around the platform, wondering why no one was getting off the train. The police arrived and tried to clear the platform; not before we had a glimpse into the train. Everyone was dead and some dismembered. Noel made sure we made a quick exit as he knew what an affect it would have on me and of course there would be a lot of disturbance. Somehow we managed to get through the crowds. Bad news spreads fast and people were amassing by the minute.

When we arrived home, I was shaking. The horror of what I saw remains a memory I want to forget.

I have recalled it here for you because it is true history.

Wellington Mall where we lived was a beautiful part of Lahore Cantonment, with tall poplar trees and wide green verges on either side of the pavement. When the army trucks brought in the refugees, they were dumped on Wellington Mall – thousands of them. They had very few belongings; just bits tied up in bundles. They had no food and no conveniences. They slept on the verges and gradually as more refugees were dumped, they infiltrated into the grounds of the houses along the Mall. It was very sad but the situation was horrendous. They were dying of cholera and my Mum would get vaccine from the hospital and go amongst them and vaccinate as many as she could. We had to stay in doors but could still see the dead bodies. Eventually trucks came everyday and piled the bodies into the trucks to dispose of them. This went on for about three weeks and then the army came to collect the survivors and took them off. I am not sure where they went but at least I felt they would now be sheltered and fed.

The above is a tiny bit of the horrors that occurred because of the partitioning of the subcontinent. I am thankful this particular part of my manuscript has come to an end.

We make a living by what we get, but we make a life by what we give.

Winston Churchill

Chapter Six

Elston-Green Ancestry

My dear Grandchildren

As I suspect you are curious, a trait which is ubiquitous in our genetic makeup, I will try to be thorough and tell you all I can about us; your family and mine.

It is difficult to give you a correct family tree of the Elston-Greens because they were Roman Catholic and the Catholics did not register births, baptisms, marriages and deaths in the civil registry but only in Churches, so unless one knows the actual church, there is no trace. I can trace back to Pop's father, but that is it.

However, I have a tree that Harry compiled, but I feel the first English part is not correct but then I could be wrong so I will append it below so that the Elston-Green line will be recorded for you and perhaps if you are interested, you can further research this ancestral line. The name Green is a common name and therefore very hard to locate in the census documents. We need to have definite tie ups.

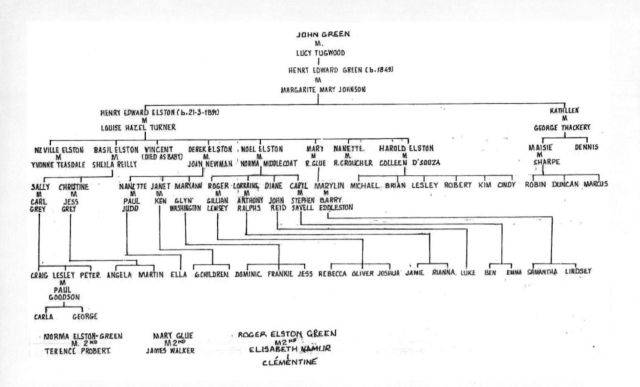

I do remember Poppy Green, (as we all called him); (Noel's Dad) telling me that his grandparents joined their names into the double barreled 'Elston-Green'. However church clerks could not absorb the 'two-tone' surname and so it has been recorded as a second name on all the certificates of the boys, rather confusing issues. Even Poppy's baptism certificate has omitted the 'Elston' in his surname, it has been registered as a second name, yet his marriage certificate has the Elston included. No one in those days ever checked or saw these records that were written by church clerks. They were kept in the church.

Poppy was an official on the Engineering side of the North Western Railway. He was a clever man, extremely good at mathematics. I have quite a few of his papers and letters, but no family tree except the one Harry did. I will insert the little that I have, if I can find something creditable, which will encompass the Elston-Green line. Poppy was a saint! I say this because he deserves to be canonized in my opinion anyway. A truly wonderful human being whom we all adored. Louisa Elston-Green, your great grandmother, on the other hand was not popular with her children in-law, except me. She disapproved of her other sons' wives. They had a rough time with her. Mother Green as we called her was very strong minded and quite tyrannical if she did not like anyone of her boys' choices. Luckily, she approved of me; at least to my face! She was adored by my children for sure. She and Poppy lived with us in England and both eventually died; Mother in a hospital and Pop in our home. Your parents really loved their grandparents. Mum Green didn't seem to mind her girls' partners, it was the boys who she idolized and spoiled where her objections were lodged, and she was particular about who they married. The girls married well, but Nancy had a difficult time and has spent most of her young life with her friend. Mary and Nancy were twins. They were pretty well to do and lived in large houses before Poppy left the Railway, before I knew any of them.

Wish I could write more of the Elston-Greens but apart from Derrick, my brother, and I living with them for a while and going out together with the brothers my information about them is limited. I have, however, a short narrative of their beautiful home where we all lived together for a short while but they had that home for a long time. Long before Noel and I met. Perhaps my composition below; some writing I did for an assignment, might give you a good picture of the Elston-Green boys and of their home.

Below the house that was once the Elston-Green home. Wellington Mall, Lahore Cantonments, Pakistan

I was viewing this house with my son, on a trip back to Lahore in 2006. He was seeing it for the first time. This was one of his ancestral homes and yours too. I put this in here for you, my darlings to give you a glimpse into our past. Many a happy day was spent in this house and in the gardens. Your granddad and I were both party people. The composition below is a memoir. It was entitled 'A derelict Building'

It stood there – forlorn, in a dire state of dereliction—that sad building, a house that once was a home. Where are the happy people that lived there; the children? Have the years flown by so fast? Yes they have. Sixty five years have passed since it was last seen. Of course it was in prime condition then – white and stately with a fruit orchard kept in pristine condition by the gardener. The orchard is gone. What a waste of nature's abundance.

Now look at this house – white paint turning a greyish green with mildew, the stately white pillars, still holding their regal look, but discoloured by age and neglect.

Steps running along the whole length of the veranda—once clean and white, now dirty and grey—lead down to the stone patio. Oh how cruel time can be. This patio was once a place for social gatherings and happiness and it was used at times to sleep under the stars; wide-stringed beds with cotton mattresses were preferable to sleeping indoors on hot and humid tropical nights. Now this patio is moss covered and strewn with dead foliage.

A paved driveway, elegant white gate and grounds marked by an unobtrusive, discreet, white wood fence graced this lovely house whereas now an ugly, brick wall is built high around the house, obstructing the view of grass verges and the road.

Broken slate tiles, abandoned and piled against the outside of the wall, high enough to climb and to enable one to get a better look at the house and grounds and to take photographs as keep sakes with the help of my digital camera. Why are they tearing it down? It looks sound, it is made of stone. Why can't they renovate it? This lovely house that once was a home is now desolate, the leafy foliage still embracing its stately past glory. Now it is silent and lost in time.

Whilst gazing at the house, a moment of reminiscence dawns and I see it again as it used to be. Memories come flooding back. It is yesterday again. I step back in time.

The smell of jasmine in the cool of the evening, the stone patio adorned with flower tubs, overflowing with tropical flowers and bougainvillea creepers running up the far ends of the veranda and meeting in the middle, encouraged by the gardener's loving hands, with blooms of red hanging in profusion, almost covering the stone carved trellis-worked overhang that decorated the veranda frontage; table and chairs were set on the creamy white patio for an evening drink before dinner.

'Hello, Doll, what would you like to drink?' queried Noel, one of the brothers in the Elston-Green family and my current boy friend.

'A Nimbu Pani would be nice'. I was hot because I had just arrived on my bicycle. I lived down the same tree lined avenue, a journey of about ten minutes. I tossed my brown curls and swept up my hair to expose my neck to the pedestal fan's powerful cool air stream drying the wet hair that was clinging to my neck.

Louise and Henry Elston-Green owned this house and the boys stayed with them for the time being as Noel, demobbed from the Air Force and the other two brothers from the Army and I, also demobbed from the Air Force, were in the process of looking for jobs in civilian life. The year 1945 – I was twenty and Noel twenty-one. Noel was a boxer and had been selected for the Olympics, but broke his arm before the team was due to depart.

Many happy memories are immersed within the surrounds of this now derelict house. One such memory springs to mind of Chris, Noel's niece, a three year old who rode her tricycle up and down the veranda at high speed; stopping just inches from the edge where there was a drop of about four feet. We all watched her in agitation, fearing for her safety, but she seemed to have a profound sense of judgement and her little legs would come off the pedals at a precise moment before the edge, stopping the front wheel of the trike on the edge of the veranda. Our warnings went unheeded.

It was a hot day as usual, in the early summer, with a cloudless blue sky. The sun was setting and it would soon be dark. No twilight in the tropics – just daylight and as soon as the huge red sun sank below the horizon there was darkness.

'Guess what Derek did last night?' Noel addressed me.

'What did he do – something awful no doubt?'

'He came home drunk and mistook Harry's bed for the toilet and pee-d on him. The best part is that Harry watched him and didn't stop him.' Harry was the youngest brother.

'How disgusting!' I said 'Why didn't you stop him, Harry?' I was amazed at this offence, even though Derek was drunk how could Harry endure this indignity?

'Well I heard that if you stop a person in mid pee, they get some kind of disease, so I let him finish and then went indoors, showered, changed and slept in my own bed. I thought it safer.'

'Well, Harry I think you were silly to endure it but I do think it funny' I said and laughed; the boys all joined in, including Harry.

The drinks were brought out by the *bearer* (waiter) in tall, cold glasses, frosted on the outside, filled with Tom Collins and John Collins cocktails and the famous nimbu pani in a large glass jug. Nimbu pani was the most appreciated thirst quencher on a warm steamy night. Plenty of fresh limes squeezed into a jug with a dash of salt and sugar, added to ice cubes and topped with water—the recipe for this simple drink. Separate glasses were left on the table in case anyone preferred to quench their thirst before indulging in cocktail drinking.

The conversation flowed smoothly, with anecdote after anecdote. Each Elston-Green son was gifted with a dry and wonderful sense of humour. There was plenty of laughter and banter between the boys. I joined in now and again but most of the time I just enjoyed the company while we waited for dinner to be served.

This is about the only picture I can find of Mum and Poppy Elston-Green. Pop is on and the left and Mum is on the right. It is Caryl's christening with Christine her Godmother holding Caryl and her Godfather Raymond standing behind. Roger is with his Nan.

Chapter Seven

The Middlecoat Ancestry

They were madmen; but they had in them that little flame which is not to be snuffed out.
Pierre Auguste Renoir
1841—1919

My dear Grandchildren

I will now write about yours and my family ancestry that goes beyond your parents and grandparents on the Middlecoat side of the family.

This is the Middlecoat family crest that is registered in the Book of Heraldry.

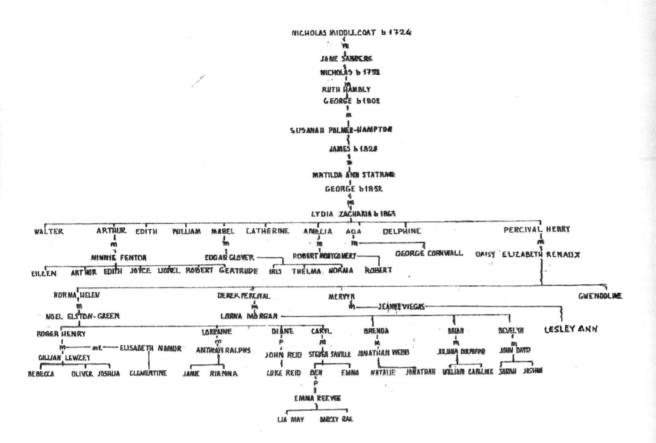

This is a rough family tree of the Middlecoat family done by Terry from information provided by Aunty Gwen and me. Anyway it will give you an idea of where you come from. Most of you are in the tree!

The one following is my mother's ancestors and yours too. You may need a magnifying glass to see these family trees.

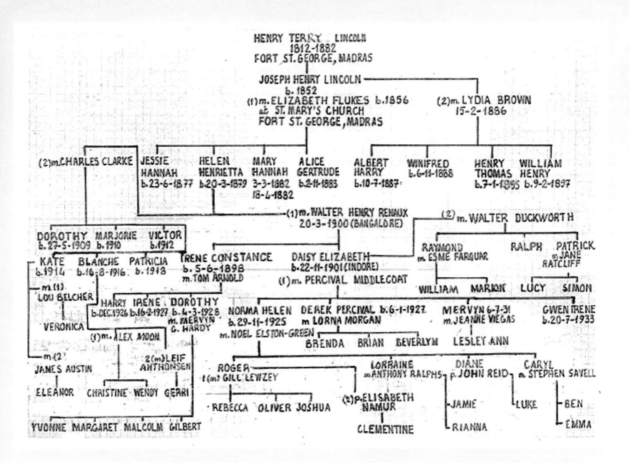

Dealing with the Middlecoats; my father, Percival Henry Middlecoat, was born in Mhow, (Rajasthan) India. He was the youngest of a family of ten. His ancestry was British military. His great, great grandfather was a Lieutenant Colonel in the British Army, who decided to domicile in India. He could well have been one of 'White Moghuls' (William Dalrymple) of India. On record, however, it was not so romantic because he was married to an Englishwoman, and so was his son, James Hampton Penson Middlecoat. They too domiciled in India but did not intermarry with Indians.

There was British lineage on my father's side of the family and French, British and Portuguese on my mother's side. Whatever they were, they were colonisers of India, and these ancestors liked India so much that they decided to stay and, no wonder, because in India they maintained the status of rajas or princes whereas in their own country they were just ordinary military or trading people.

The affluent life style of the Raj suited them. Eventually, on release from their military or trading positions they settled in India and some colonisers inter-married with native women, who were very beautiful; some from rich and noble backgrounds. In tracing a family tree one comes across amazing information like General William Palmer (mentioned earlier). Unlike The General there were some Europeans who had children out of wedlock, but because India had strict moral codes on this issue, marriage was usually the norm. The foreigners were sometimes compelled by the Indian parents to marry the women they chose as partners. Some of these women came from elite families of the country. Most of the Europeans who stayed in India were officials in the various forces, or trading companies, and were the only ones who had accumulated enough wealth, legitimately or illegitimately as the case may be, to be able to afford to do so.

Some European men married into Muslim families and chose (or were compelled) to give up their identities, their religion and their mode of dress in order to merge into the society they chose to adopt. They lived in luxury, some having more than one wife and several children. The wives brought weighty dowries into the marriage which goods, such as jewellery or money, was monopolised by the husband; normal according to British law in India.

To get back to our line of descendants, James Hampton Pinson or Penson, (we are not one hundred per cent sure which name is correct) Middlecoat had a son, another George, Percy's father, and my grandfather (your great, great grandfather), George Statham Penson Middlecoat seemed to break the Middlecoat mould and did not marry an English woman, but married Lydia Zacharias, who, according to the records kept, is referred to as a 'native of India'? I like to think that this is where our Indian blood comes from but after talking to an official in the British Library Records Office in London, it may not be so because, as I was informed, 'native of India' could mean that she lived or domiciled in India. She does not appear to have been educated because her signature just says 'Lydia' or a mark something like it. It is stated that Lydia was a Christian.

It is sad that we cannot find out anything more about her. All we do know is that she died after my father's birth, her tenth child by George Statham and it is rumoured that she died of cholera. However, this is word of mouth information. I know that my father never spoke of her, perhaps because he never knew her. His sisters brought him up. Though there are many pictures of George with members of the family. He did appear to remain in close contact with his daughters and must have been in my father's life though I do not recall my Dad speaking of his father.

The main reason I am writing this manuscript is because there are so few of this generation left who can tell you anything at all about your lineage or about the land that is your heritage through you lineage.

There must have been something special about Lydia because George stayed with her till her death and the ten children they produced together were all duly recorded as being baptised in the Anglican Church. All that is, except my Dad, Percy, who was her last child. His baptism is not recorded. Maybe because his mother died and she must have been the religious one. Anyway he, my Dad that is, was not at all religious as far as I can remember. I don't ever remember him going to church as our friends' parents did.

Reading this genealogy history one realises that there were some couples who were unmarried but lived for many years with the same person, hence the offspring were produced out of wedlock. Now this goes back to the 1700's and 1800's. This as it happens was not only the norm with Euro/Indian couples, but Europeans in the Victorian era as well. Research has proven that if a married couple did not get along, and as divorce was almost impossible, and if the partnership did not bring happiness and compatibility, they terminated the relationship and moved into one they preferred!

It is quite interesting to know that marriage during those years was not of primary importance. Loyalty and love seemed to be the staying power in relationships.

My father, Percy, your great grandfather was, as were all his family members, well educated. He was a literary man. I remember him reading me bits of Byron's canto, 'Don Juan' when I was about ten! He was like me in that respect, trying desperately to impart his literary knowledge to his then 'unwilling to listen' daughter. He read me many literary passages from the books he read, but Byron sticks out in my mind because he loved Byron's satirical poetry. It was lost on me then, but ironically, that canto was one of my last assignments when I studied the Romantic Poets. I wish I had listened to my father's instructions.

There is much I remember about him. He influenced my life because I loved him deeply. I was a bit young to appreciate his taste in literature, but I did try hard to absorb what he was trying to impart to me. It must surely have been my father's influence that made me seek knowledge so avidly throughout my life; in particular, literature.

Another bit of information about my Dad that sticks in my mind is that he was a speed freak! He had a fast motorbike (fast for those years of the 1930's – I think it was a Norton). He also had a sports car – weird to look at now, but very few people had cars in those days and my Dad was always one for the best. He was known as 'Speed King Percy' because he drove his mail train from Peshawar, in the North West Frontier, to Lahore in the Punjab, at a record speed that no one could beat in his life time. Those were the days of the big, shiny, steam locomotives that were the pride and joy of their drivers. The driver's firemen and staff had to shine those engines until they gleamed, the brass work polished so that one could see one's face reflected. His title was associated too with his love of speed on any moving vehicle.

My Dad's father, George Statham, must have been the black sheep in the Middlecoat family. Researching his records in the British Library showed him to have different professions at different times. We have discovered that the Middlecoats had money, which all the sons inherited. They owned land in Britain and India. In Mhow they had property called 'Rose Villa Gardens' that the Middlecoats inherited through marriage. I am told that there was a long driveway into the property with rose gardens on either side and the land contained orchards and extensive grounds. I understand from a distant relative that the property is now derelict and neglected.

I have an ancient photograph of one of my father's sister's houses which I will append below. The snapshot is extremely old but will give you an idea of the size of their homes.

An extremely faded and torn picture depicting part of my aunt's Ada's home – the two men on the left are George Statham Middlecoat the other his son in law, the lady in the doorway is my aunt. The man in front must be a servant. No one is sure of his status.

Below is a picture of my first cousin who was 16 when I was 8 and I adored him. He was very sweet and patient with me, and always had time to talk to me. I stayed with my Aunt and Uncle on occasion and Robert was in and out of the house. Well here he is—my first heart throb.

Above is a picture of George, my Granddad (second from right – back row) extreme right is my very tall Uncle Glover and extreme left is my Daddy! The ladies in front are Aunts and the children are cousins. There were eventually six of them. The couple getting married are Robert's parents. Robert and I were not even thought of when this was taken.

This will give you an idea of my father's side of the family who are your ancestors.

I often stayed with the Glovers. My Aunt was tiny and he was very tall. She was dominant and tried to boss him about. He used to pick her up and put her on top of the tall boy, the furniture in India was really big, and leave her there until she capitulated for whatever reason was pertinent at the time. I remember him; he was a fun loving person. He was English, and an Army officer. This story was told to me by a cousin about my aunt. I never actually witnessed it.

A can of worms has been opened through our research into my mother's family background. Do not get me wrong, my mother was legitimately born in wedlock so was her older sister, Irene. Her father was French, and he and my grandmother were married but separated when my mum, Daisy, was about seven. All I know is what my mother told me and that was that my grandfather would not give my grandmother a divorce. My Granny then partnered Charles Clarke. Charles was a Freemason and may have married my grandmother in some Masonic form but I have no idea. There is no record of any marriage. My cousins and I find it is quite ironic because my aunts (mother's sisters) were snobbish because of their affluent life style and because they looked English. They never knew till a few years ago. My aunt Dorothy who lived in Canada to the age of one hundred years, sadly died last year. My Aunt Blanche died this year (2011) at the age of ninety-five. Neither would openly discuss India in front of their nieces, probably not even between themselves. They lived a great life in India, England, Norway and Canada. They were white and so they put India off the map for themselves and their children. They lived an illusion. Like quite a few Anglo Indians, they were ashamed of their Indian ancestry. I called my Aunt Dorothy who is older, 'the Queen' and my Aunt Blanche, 'the Duchess'. They were quite regal in their bearing even in old age. The other sisters and mum's brother are all dead now. My cousins, now that they know about it, embrace their Indian heritage in spite of the fact that their parents disowned it.

My cousins and I have opened the can of worms, but this archival information is totally interesting to them. In fact, they find it quite comical and farcical. Who cares any more whether people are married or not? Obviously they did not care much is the 1800's either.

However my mum told me that when I was a few months old, her father, Henry Renaux, returned to see her and me. She said he was very emotional and cried while he held us both in his arms. The good thing is he gave my grandmother a divorce, a bit late as some of the children were around by then. My Gran was a wonderful woman and came from a very musical and talented family. Her father was English and was the band leader of the Governor's band in Fort St George. On his papers he is known as 'First Class Musician'. One of Granny's sisters was a concert pianist. My cousins on my mother's side of the family seem to be gifted musicians and singers. One of my uncles or great uncles was a famous banjo player.

Fort St George was a British stronghold and was exclusively British. My grandmother was born, baptised and married her French husband, Henry Walter Renaux outside of Fort St George. The British and French were not good friends at that time as they were always battling over land in India. I have all her documents.

Below is a painting of the famous Fort St George near Madras in the days of the East India Company:

My two aunts, Dorothy and Blanche, were quite regal in their bearing and had clear, lucid minds that absorbed world affairs and everything about people around them. They dressed with great style and liked all the good things in life. They conversed well and intelligently and were in no way old except for the number of years they had lived. I saw them both when I visited Canada a few years before they died.

My Granny and Granddad Clarke were very loved by us children probably because they loved and spoiled us. We often went on holiday to their home in Karachi. They did live in Rawalpindi when we were there and we lived in the same town. I for one remember their huge home. My Gran loved chickens and ducks (as pets—not for eating!). Well to get back to their home in Karachi, I remember my aunts and uncle. However, my most vivid memories are of my glamorous aunts. They were always going to dances and parties and I loved to watch them in their party dresses.

granny + Granddad Clarke

My Gran and Granddad Clarke

This is my real French Granddad, Henry Renaux and his second wife.
They owned three tea plantations, one in Sri Lanka and two in the mountains somewhere.

Holly, my mother's half sister. Her parents are the two above.

My mum had an older sister, Irene, who was slightly crippled and who stayed at home to look after her younger siblings. We have no pictures of Irene, nor does her daughter, my cousin because Irene died after giving birth to her.

Mum, left home very young, about seventeen because my granddad did not approve of my father because he had dark skin. He was a student at the time, so Mum became a nurse and lived in the hospital. Dad and Mum did not see each other very often as they lived far apart from each other. She and Dad married when she was 23 and he was 35.

When I visited my Aunt Dorothy in Canada, she told me something about my mother in her young years that I knew nothing of. Mum was very musical, played the piano and was always singing. Aunt said that Mum was the life of the family, full of fun and always happy. When Mum took her siblings to the park Aunt Dorothy told me that all the boys were attracted to Mum, but she (Dorothy) was very timid and would not go and play with the children, but would hang on to Mum's skirt and never give her a chance to be with the boys. She also said that Mum never scolded her or complained.

My mother was an angel throughout her life, but an angel with great spiritual fire in every sense of the word. If she was crossed, then one would see the fire! However she loved people and people the world over loved her.

I have Noel's birth certificate, his father, Henry's, baptism and Henry and Louise's marriage document. Her real name was Louisa but everyone called her Lou of Louise. Poppy (that is what we all called Noel's father) told me that his parents combined their surnames and made it into Elston-Green. The clerks who filled in Church registers in India could not understand this and the Elston was written on all their baptism certificates as a second name. As if a mother would give the same second name to all her sons! In India, when a child is baptized or confirmed, a marriage certificate of the parents has to be provided and sometimes the church demands to see the grandparents' certificates too of the child concerned hence, we have names copied incorrectly and names heard incorrectly. The Catholic Church can really complicate things!

When I was eleven years old, my father died on New Years day in 1936. He ran in a race on Christmas day at the Club and refused to put his coat back on. It was cold in Rawalpindi in December. He caught cold which developed into pneumonia – a dreaded disease in those days before antibiotics – and so the father that was my inspiration and mentor left me and my heart was broken, as was my mother's. Boys just don't fret for long it seems, but I did. My Dad's sisters came and so did my mother's family. None of us children were allowed to go to the funeral. We stayed with friends for the day. They had boys and my brothers and the boys played together, whilst I draped myself on the fence to watch the funeral procession go by. I felt very deserted because my Dad and I had a special bond.

This is a picture of my Dad with Rover our spaniel.

I have not written much about my sister Gwen so below is a story that I think you will all find interesting and very funny too in part. Again it is a composition of mine that I wrote a long time ago and it is written in the present tense.

My Sister – The Nun

She is named Gwen—this pretty, blonde haired, blue eyed baby is there for me. After only having brothers I claim her as mine. The year is 1934.

When she is in her fourth year, our adored father dies and leaves us. We are all very sad.

I am in my eleventh year in boarding school in Murree in the foothills of the Himalayas. Our school is a real beauty spot, pine forests and large coniferous trees surround the school, with monkeys, leopards and birds that live in the forests. The smell of pines mixed with exotic, mountain flowers add to this profusion of beauty and perfume. The school is safely fenced off, so the animals and the children are kept well apart. But there is no Gwen here.

It is now the month of March 1938 and the ground is covered in soft and fluffy snow, about three to four feet deep. The heavy snowfall in the winter months is the norm. The drive and pathway is cleared.

Because of my father's sudden death, my mother has to work and so Gwen and my young brother, Mervyn, are sent to the nursery in my school as boarders on a temporary basis. I am overjoyed.

School days are good times for us. Gwen grows into a lovely little girl but the day arrives when Mum remarries and she and Mervyn leave for home in Rawalpindi, very near the present capital city of Pakistan, Islamabad.

As we grow and develop, Gwen and I are very close. She follows me everywhere and copies all I do. She is, however, influenced by a Catholic lady who lives near us. Gwen is encouraged at the tender age of seven to go to the Catholic Church with her. Our family except for my step father is Anglican. Gwen fusses until she is allowed to convert to Catholicism and she is instrumental in converting Mervyn and my mother too. My older brother and I remain staunch Anglicans.

As a teenager Gwen is a pupil in a Convent boarding school. Our schools are in the same town. Later my brother (17) and I (19) also convert to Catholicism with her influence and that of the man I eventually married. This, however, is not my story—it is Gwen's.

On leaving school she announces to the family that she intends to become a teaching nun. We are astounded and feel she is deserting us.

Gwen is beautiful. Her baby blonde hair is now a rich dark/auburn brown and her eyes reflect the colour she wears, sometime blue, sometimes green and at other times blue-grey. It is a shame that all this beauty will be hidden by a veil and a nun's habit.

She obtains her BA and B-ED degrees and is soon an exceptionally good teaching nun. In time she becomes a Reverend Mother. Her new name is Sister Margaret Mary.

She lives in a sheltered environment and I live in the real world. She is temperate and mild in disposition. I am wild and passionate with a volatile disposition. Though we are not at all alike we are close and agree to disagree on many points. We are like parallel lines that run along side each other, staying ever close but never really meeting. We are separate individuals.

Eventually Gwen is given a village appointment. She is an excellent organizer; practical and skillful. She is artistic and architectural, hence her appointment to supervise the building of a school and a church in Mariakhel, a village in the Thal desert of Pakistan, and to run the school as Principal. This is no mean task and the fact that she is chosen to accomplish it amazes me. My little sister, who was my shadow, has now overshadowed me—in a different aspect of life no doubt.

In a couple of years her desert blooms. A school is built with housing for nuns and guests and classrooms for the children she hopes will come. A church with accommodation for the clergy is erected. The project is modern and a total marvel. There are orchards of orange, lemon, apricot, pumlo and other fruit trees. A large vegetable garden produces an abundance of crops and exotic flower gardens enhance the buildings. Meat is supplied by the village farmers and their hunter priest.

Even though the area is a desert the soil is arable. Just below the surface there is water, which is obtained through the drilling of tube wells. The water is pure and cold. The orchards and gardens are watered by outside pumps and inside the building plumbing supplies running water and water closets.

The village people, Muslims mostly, are wary of the religious and the convent. Before long, however, they are captivated by Gwen's and the other nuns' outgoing sweetness and kindness to them. Eventually the school is full of students, not necessarily Catholic though some do convert. Education is the primary goal and this is entirely successful.

With all this talent, Gwen is naïve. One day a wild boar attacked two villagers and killed one. It had been wounded by a hunter's bullet and was out for revenge against mankind.

Gwen is in her vegetable garden when this wild boar stands on the opposite side to her, menacing, panting, grunting, frothing at the mouth and bleeding. Gwen looks at the boar

'Poor little piggy – who has hurt you?'

She has a soft, soothing voice. With this she reaches out her hand with the green cabbage to this infuriated wild beast.

'Piggy' stood there looking at her in seeming amazement. Here is someone who is not threatening him, nor firing a gun at him and offering him green cabbage to eat. He truly is confused. Gwen, or Sister Margaret Mary as she is now called, is in grave danger but she is totally oblivious to it, all she wants is to comfort and console this wounded animal. It stands there immobile, looking at her and its pants and grunts gradually subside; it begins to relax when suddenly the Catholic priest (the hunter), the village headman and his henchman arrive with their guns, followed by many others with latis (large sticks) and they shoot the boar. Sister Margate Mary is furious.

'How dare you shoot this poor pig in my garden?' She rants at them as they try to explain the necessity to destroy him and also to placate her wrath.

When the pig is presented to the school and the priest as a gift, Sister Margaret Mary refuses to even look at the succulent dish that is prepared and that all enjoy. The aromatic smell permeates the air but she thinks it a sacrilege.

On another occasion a fête is held in the village. The younger nuns obtain what they think are good value balloons from a shopkeeper.

The 'balloons' are blown up and are being sold at the fête when after a while the priest notices them and with horror talks quietly to Gwen. The simple village children are buying balloons and they are all over the grounds. Parents and others are giggling. Gwen is extremely embarrassed when she has to tell her nuns that they are selling condoms! There is consternation and confusion as all the balloons have to be burst and money refunded to bring normality back to the village fête.

This then is the life my sister chooses. Cloistered and dull? I do not think so. Fulfilling and interesting? Yes, indeed.

Proper words in proper places make the true definition of a style.
Jonathan Swift

Chapter Eight

Himalayas and their Foothill Towns

My dear Grandchildren

This is a poem I wrote some years ago. I think you will see how very much these beautiful mountains mean to me; how they inspired me just to gaze up at them and to live in the valleys of some of the highest peaks in the world. I include this poem in my manuscript because it is my composition and describes the high peaks of this amazing range of mountains; often referred to as the roof of the world.

Himalayas
By Helen Renaux

How tempting, how luring—you snowbound peaks!
Reaching high up into the cloudless, sky—
Roof of the world you're called; no wonder why
As sunlight paints your peaks with golden streaks
While the vales beneath you in darkness lie.
At first light of dawn your tips catch the sun;
High, high above this cold, snow covered earth
When continents crashed to first give you birth.

Gazing at you from green valleys below;
Remote and inaccessible you seem;
And yet—your peaks have been conquered so
Many a time by man—your lure extreme
Beguiles and pulls him to challenge you;
Your inhospitable ice slopes he braves
To suffer pain; frostbite and sometimes too
To lose life; to lie buried in icy caves.

A sudden, swift, swirl of a wispy cloud
Encircles and crowns your celestial height
With sun kissed glory; you stand tall, erect
Haloed for a moment; a hallowed sight;
You are oblivious of this effect
Yet, not mortal man: who looks up in awe
At a wondrous sight of a peak lit bright
Tempting and luring—to climb as before.

The elegant lammergeyers don't try
To reach your peaks even though they can fly,
Higher than most; the griffin vulture can
Glide effortlessly too with its wing span
Silhouetted against the glacial fall
Of ice rock faces in their soaring thrall;
These birds of prey despite their skill and might
Do not attempt to reach your awesome height.

Yet man—who walks but upon his two feet
Will scale your cruel face and toil and beat
The terror of your dreadful slopes to reach
Your seeming insurmountable peak.
Mans' indomitable will defeats you,
To gain pre-eminence; to attain his dream;
To conquer you and to join you in your
Majesty; there to share your reign supreme.

This part of my narrative will tell you about the geography and history of the towns I loved, beginning with the mountain area of the North. These places are very much a part of me, and therefore a part of your family heritage. I think Roger is the only one besides me that has visited briefly in this beautiful area.

The small towns that nestled among lush, green pines in the foothills of the Himalayan Mountains, the Hindu Kush and the Karakoram ranges, were called hill stations. Calling them 'hill stations' was ludicrous really, because what we call hills in United Kingdom would be considered, by contrast in Himalayan terms, hillocks or mounds! However, let's not put our UK landscape down because we have our own beauty in the Lake District, the Peak District, Snowdonia and the Scottish Highlands where the hills are gentle and rounded, heather clad in autumn and sometimes steep and rugged but no less beautiful; just different.

In the Himalayan foothills we have high mountainous terrain, jagged and steep in some places and in the lower elevations (well over 1,000 meters), thickly pine forested with exotic flowers and fauna, hardly 'hills' as they were referred to in English terminology. They were mountains. The air was clear and fresh. There was no pollution because cars were not allowed further than a certain height, and probably could not make it up the steep climbs. I am talking about my young days, hence I am now writing in the past tense, when the school children had rosy red cheeks and lips and their eyes shone with health and well being. Even the coolies who carried up some of our luggage had shiny red cheeks. Since those days, the mountains have been excavated to make roads that are now extended to run quite high up into the 'hills' and the schools are now accessible by car.

I spent most of my early years in two of these hill stations, Murree and Abbottabad. Abbottabad, situated in the District of Hazara, was named after James Abbott who founded it as a military camp in 1853. Abbott was the first Deputy Commissioner of the Hazara District during the British Raj.

The discovery of coins of the Greco-Bectrian kings discovered in this district, seem to suggest that the area was inhabited in the first century B.C.

Abbottabad was a smallish town from which you could see the most stunning scenic beauty in Pakistan; surrounded by lofty peaks, and pine scented air that permeated everything. Some of the hill stations were deserted during winter months, but Abbottabad was always a favourite spot, with its bracing weather. It was lively all year round, with beautiful gardens and roadways within the town, lined with tall trees. There were stretches of green turf with plenty of room for polo or football matches, or hockey, cricket and golf; somewhat a sportsman's paradise. Abbottabad is situated at about 1,250 meters above sea level. Murree reaches over 2,743 meters in some places and on the whole, Murree was situated on a higher elevation than Abbottabad although slightly further south geographically.

Abbottabad, like Shrinagar in Kashmir, is situated in a valley surrounded by towering mountain peaks whereas Murree is mountainous and referred to as Murree Hills, and wherever one trod in Murree; one was either climbing or descending. From Kashmir Point, the highest point in Murree, to the Gali's or valleys, the view of the towering, year round, snowcapped mountain peaks was visible on clear days.

I can even to this day close my eyes and see a mental vision of those glorious peaks in the distance and almost hear the sounds of the wildlife in the evergreen forests; all sorts of exotic birds and animals that roamed outside of and within the confines of the hill stations. Through my mind's eye I can see the camel caravans that used the then Silk Road to pass through Abbottabad. My young life in the mountains was so impressive and is imprinted in my memory. I can recall many minute details of my school days and the various returns I made to Murree and Abbottabad as a young woman. The caravan cavalcades were one of those impressive memories. It was from one such as these that I bought my dog, Spotty for five rupees and also my donkey, Rastas who I mentioned earlier on. I called my dog 'Spotty' because her real name was unpronounceable to me. Spotty was quite an entertainer, she was white with black spots; probably a dalmatian and terrier mix. She stayed with me in the teacher's house at Burn Hall (where I taught for a few years) and she became a favorite with the teachers and the children. She was a show off (dalmation trait) and could do many tricks; she could be vindictive (a terrier trait) and she was averse to men wearing *salwars* (baggy trousers). I'm not sure if she hated the men or the trousers. She never got over this, even after I left home and she became the family pet.

Whilst I am on the topic of Abbottabad and Murree I will introduce here, because it took place in Abbottabad, some of your near ancestors and snippets of the grandfather none of you had the pleasure of knowing.

Noel used to visit me in Abbottabad, even though I left Lahore because of him. I broke off our relationship and moved to Abbottabad to put distance between us and to teach. Noel was dogged in his pursuit of me. He did not understand nor accept the word 'no'.

On one memorable occasion Mary (Noel's sister), her husband, Sticky Glue (the nick name is obvious) and I, clad in thick sheepskin jackets went into the pine woods collecting cones in pillow cases on a cold winter's day in the village of Shinkiari near Abbottabad. Shinkiari was a pretty little place. It had a dried up river bed which was awash with Oleander bushes which stretched for miles. The blossoms were red and pink; a beautiful sight to see. Shinkiari was thickly pine forested. Most of the forested areas were full of evergreens but there were also many chestnut trees.

This is where Mary and Sticky lived with their baby, Marilyn. We carried home the pine cones we collected and put them on the roaring fire in the lounge and we feasted on roasted marshmallows and chestnuts after dinner. The aroma from the pine cones, sparkling and glowing in the flames, wafted through the house. It was a very happy time for all of us and this little memory sticks solidly in my mind. Noel often came to Abbottabad and spent time with his sister. Mary and Noel had a very close relationship.

Mary was attractive; small with brown hair and brown eyes. She had a lively, dry sense of humour. She loved to party and drink. She and I got on well and I loved being with her and Sticky. His real name was Raymond but no one I know called him that. He was tall, good looking, with light hair and a calm and placid disposition. He was a Major in the Army. They took me to various places outside of Shinkiari and Abbottabad. I met many officers and had a wonderful time.

Another occasion that is worth recounting is when Mary and I were chased by bulls. We decided not to take Marilyn and pram and left her with the ayah and decided to walk to Sticky's Army Office, a few miles towards Abbottabad and we took the dogs; two German Shepherds, one was called 'Mary Glue' who was a terror and decided to incite the herd, snapping at their legs. Eventually the bulls became furious and decided to give chase. Mary and I ran because we were truly in the line of the stampede and I jumped into an army truck that was nearby. My companion, not so agile, got under it. The dogs followed, barking and snapping. The bulls were butting the truck and trying to attack all and sundry. All I remember is the truck being rocked and battered. I was very concerned about Mary who was under it and out of my sight. However, the bulls fortunately became bored with the proceedings and wandered off back to their field. Mary crawled out from under the truck. She looked a mess, with bits of hay and other debris in her hair. We were both shaken with the experience, but when I looked at her with her hands on her hips glaring in the direction of the herd in the field. I could not control my laughter, whether through release of tension or just because it was funny, Mary joined in and we both became hysterically stupid and could not stop laughing. It was one of those silly situations when one looks at another after a silly happening and giggles just cannot be suppressed. However we eventually calmed down and continued our trip, shaken but safe. Needless to say we headed straight for the officers mess and the bar.

One of Noel's brothers, Harry, was also posted in Abbottabad. He was an Army officer and we were together in Abbottabad for about a year and the two of us had a wonderful time together. This was before Noel and I were married. Harry was great fun. He looked a bit like Noel and had his charm and sense of humour but that however is where the resemblance ended. Noel was tough, moody and could be aggressive whereas Harry was all charm and gentleness. We got on well together and had a few dinners in the Officers' Mess. It was a happy time to remember.

Our family would get together on many an occasion for a sing song when Dad visited and would play the guitar, or one of several instruments he could play. He was still in the army and Mum was the matron of Burn Hall boarding school. We would sing all the old tunes that Dad liked and some that we liked. I am now referring to my step-father, Walter Duckworth, who brought me up most of my life after my dad died at the age of 48 when I was eleven. Walter married my mum a year later and was our dad from them on.

Another anecdote that needs a mention is this. We were a sort of good Catholic family at that time and Mummy tried to get us to say the family rosary together, because the church slogan at the time was 'A family who prays together stays together'. Kneeling there with all good intentions at the start of our prayers and with our rosaries in our hands, heads bowed, we were good and dutiful children, praying most sincerely as only children can pray. Well, mother's efforts came to no avail, because my brother, Mervyn who was about 16 or 17 and who later joined the air force to become a great hero, began to giggle half way through the reciting of the rosary and that got us all going every day. Mum was cross with us and told us we were behaving like stupid ignorant children. I was just passed twenty one, but was considered just as guilty as the rest. My brother said he didn't do it on purpose, the giggles just came out. 'The Family Rosary' was eventually abandoned. I think all of us siblings remember this incident.

Stepping forward in time now, just for a bit, but it is relevant so please be patient and read on.

When I returned to Murree and Abbottabad in the year 2000 it deeply saddened me to see that the thick forests of my youth had become less dense. The trees had been chopped down and used for fire wood, furniture making and various other commercial ventures, I suppose. Clearing had also facilitated the building of hotels and other accommodation. The monkeys had all but disappeared; forced to the higher elevations along with the leopards and other wild creatures. Hunting and poaching also tragically reduced the leopard population, although these practices are strictly prohibited by the Pakistan eco-preserving authorities today. The displaced leopards which I remember are not to be confused with their cousins, the snow leopards, who have always populated the higher mountain ranges. I thought you might be interested in this recent article I found about the hill leopards plus a picture of a few remaining monkeys:

'There have been many instances of leopard sightings in Murree. Last year, I personally witnessed a leopard on the Jheekagali-Kuldana *Kashmir Point hiking track in Murree hills. Signboards were later placed on nearby trees to warn hikers. On a recent visit to the same spot, the leopard roar was heard again and fresh paw prints in the mud were observed as well. Although there have been no reported leopard attacks on humans in Murree hills yet, but as prudent practice the hikers in the forests should walk in groups as opposed to being alone. One should be especially careful when there are women and children around because the behavior of the leopard that attacked six women at Bakot showed a tendency towards attacking lone females.'

* The spot that is mentioned was very near to my school.

There are also many new hotels and houses being built for the people who come to these hill stations to escape the heat of the plains. They are now tourist resorts and it is sad to see some of these modern buildings side by side with the quaint buildings that existed in my youth, buildings that fitted so perfectly in the setting of these beautiful hill stations. They were peak roofed and quaint, resembling chalets in the Swiss and French Alps; some with green and red roofs and many log cabins.

Whilst in Abbottabad in my youth, friends also took me to visit Hunza, Gilgit, Swat, Chitral, Skardu (a couple of these hill towns were famous for polo), and Indus Kohistan in the Karakorum Range. All these amazing places are not too far distant from Abbottabad, the center point of the area. I have attached a couple of maps for your information. Pakistan is a vast country and when I say 'places are not too far distant' I mean you need to travel for two or three days, with stops overnight. It was very adventurous driving on these roads and I loved the excitement of travel through beautiful mountain passes and on treacherous roads, usually in some army jeep of truck.

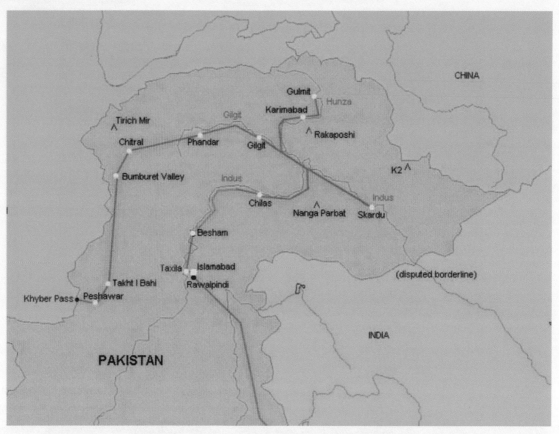

Abbottabad is somewhere between Besham and Islamabad but the distances are so vast that I cannot locate it precisely. I know we could see Tirich Mir and sometimes Rakaposhi or Nanga Parbat on clear days; three of the very high mountains of Pakistan. Pakistan has seven of the highest mountains in the world.

Baramula in the map below is in the disputed area of Kashmir and is where Granddad Noel went to school.

Not sure about you but I am a map-mad person. I love maps. Perhaps you will need a magnifying glass to see some of the towns that is if you are interested.

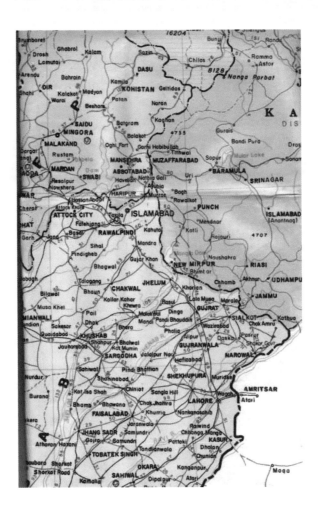

The maps above will give you an idea of the geography of some towns I mention. The Tarbela Dam is a place that your Granddad worked on at one time and then on to the Mangla Dam. He was in Ground Water Engineering at the time, before he became an oil well drilling engineer.

Abbottabad was a lovely vacation spot in the old days when I was teaching there. I understand that it is still the same today.

Now it is a world famous place because it is where Osama Bin Laden was traced to and killed by the Americans.

I notice they now spell Abbottabad with one't' but at least they still keep the name. Sargodha is where your Uncle Mervyn was based when he flew Saber Jets in the Pakistan Air Force. He was a Squadron Leader when he was in Sargodha.

Picture of my jet ace brother Mervyn, taken in Texas I think.

Now here is something of interest perhaps to the sportsmen in the family. Although I don't think there were any polo players amongst us but we are from a sports participating and sports loving family and it was a popular game. This next article shows how Pakistan is 'up' in the game of polo, with the highest polo ground in the world. Lahore was famous for polo played with 'no holds barred'. It was furious and fierce and very exciting to watch. Noel and I used to watch the matches played in the *Durbar* in Lahore. For lack of a better translation of this event, I think 'unusual sporting festival' will have to do.

They also had camel racing and bull displays, showing huge bulls with head dresses and lace shawls draped over them. They were magnificent animals owned and bred in various princely estates. Then there was bullock cart racing and horse racing with horseman who had lances and who had to pick up a small stuffed bag (for a better word) at high speed. Well here is a picture of a game of polo in progress at the highest polo field in the world and an article on polo:

The Highest Polo ground in the world

Polo is one of the oldest sports in the world. It combines the skills of the rider with the power of the horse as well as team tactics. It is played in 48 countries in 5 continents. The ancient grounds of polo stretched from Constantinople (Istanbul) to Japan during the Middle Ages. It was begun several thousand years ago as military training for the elite Sultan's army—possibly from Persia, although Pakistanis and Indians believe it originates from the Northern Areas of the subcontinent of India. The very name 'polo' is the Balti term for ball. The original teams would have been armies with dozens on each side, ready to do battle. During the world's first tournament in 600BC the Turks thrashed the Persians and the battle has continued on to this day.

The first written rules of modern Polo were created by an Irishman, Captain John Watson in 1874, where the 'offside' rule was set in stone but little understood! It was around this time that Polo was brought to the West after military colonialists discovered the game in India and it soon became a firm favourite with the aristocracy. The British Raj formed the oldest active club in the world in Calcutta. Although dropped from the official games since World War I, polo is now back on the menu as an Olympic sport. The leaders in the field are currently Argentina, the USA and England.

Rules of polo

Each team has six players, six ponies, six mallets and one ball between the two teams. The opposing teams charge their rivals and at the half way line try and score into the opposition's goal. There is much hanging off the side of the pony, smacking together of mallets and general misdemeanor. Imagine croquet on horseback without the tea and scones. The game is over when one team reaches nine goals, although modern games are more often two sides of 30 minutes.

If you're now imagining England's Prince Charles bouncing about on a horse, think again, Pakistani Polo is the real deal, aggressive, fiery and fast paced—no 'niceties'.

Let the battle commence!

A polo legend from ancient North Pakistan was that a king begged the gods to return his missing wife. The gods said they would do this, but only on the condition that he sacrifice his two sons. They gave him a powerful horse, so fast it split valleys in two on its flight to Baltistan. He smacked the heads of his sacrificed sons in to the opening in the mountain in order to reclaim his queen. Near **Kaphulu**, you can see an opening in a mountain and a real polo field where gory scenes are periodically carried out in the name of the sport. Animal heads have been used in the past as well as the severed heads of the enemies of Genghis Khan! The animals aren't the only casualties in the wild Indian style of play—even in officious matches players will try and thwack the shoulders and arms off their opponents. Half time is less slices of oranges and more time for splints and bandages. A handicap in Indian/Pakistan Polo can have quite an unpleasant connotation.

Where to see a polo match. Key tournaments of the season are the **Uprising Day** tournament *in early November in Gilgit or the **Pakistan Independence Day** tournament in Skardu in early August.*

Polo between heaven and hell

*The greatest and most infamous polo tournaments, however, takes places annually on the **Shandur Pass**, the highest polo ground in the world where a Chitral versus Gilgit tournament is held every June. The rules of the game here date back 800 years to those created by a descendent of Genghis Khan himself. The competition was created in the 1920s to promote integration between the various tribes and the British rulers. The Shandur Pass was picked as the location because, at 11,000 ft above sea level, it was seen as a ridge between heaven and hell. The loose rules practiced are, however, more likely to lead to total anarchy than integration and every year players faced injury and even death during the tournament.*

Its no casual sightseeing affair—to even get to this ground you face a 13 hour drive from Gilgit along a treacherously dangerous and narrow mountain pass where you risk possible death if you meet another jeep on the other side of the Pass! Even the ponies face a 5 day trek before the match. All in all, the fatalities are high before the match has even began, although around 10,000 polo impassioned players are prepared to make the trek out to Shandur every year. Violence, tension and corruption are all in play—and that's just off the pitch!

Noel and I loved polo hence this article is included with the hope that you may feel something of the buzz that your Granddad and I got out of this amazing game. It is now the game of princes and the upper classes. I suppose it was in those days too.

Now I am skipping ahead because I am writing about my visit to Abbottabad and Murree in 2000 and here are pictures of Burn Hall, the school I taught in (now a girl's college), and the new boy's school. The year of these pictures is the opening of the millennium – 2000.

I loved my visit to these towns of my youth and I am ever grateful to the lovely people who made it possible. One of my best friends in school was a very aristocratic Muslim girl – it was her son's wife who drove me to Abbottabad from Islamabad, and both of them took me to Murree, with Musharraf, the wife, driving. Mujtaba, the son who can drive, finds most cars restrictive because of his height. He is a Pathan and is well over 6 feet! They have three sons and a daughter. I never met the girl, but the sons were really lovely. Two of them over six feet like their Dad; very modern and well educated. One of them wrote a poem for me – this talent inherited, I suppose, from Mujtaba's sister, Rabia, who was a university professor and wrote poetry. She dedicated her handwritten document of about fifty odd poems to me just before her death a couple of years ago. Some day I will do something with them. She wanted me to edit these poems and use them in what ever way I thought fit.

To continue with my year 2000 visit to Abbottabad, Rafia's (Mujtaba's sister) brother in law, Colonel Khizar Niazi, hosted us in their lovely home and showed us all around Abbottabad. It was a sentimental journey for me. The Principal of Burn Hall School in Abbottabad, another Army Colonel, welcomed me and served me in high style, English tea in his office – a custom still maintained in the hill stations. A *bearer* (waiter) brought in a silver tray, with silver accessories such as tea pot, sugar and milk containers, a tiered cake stand holding a variety of cakes, biscuits, cake forks, silver platters with doilies, containing delicate cucumber sandwiches and the best English china. This was a real throwback to the days of the Raj. It was all so English and extremely elegant. The Colonel was completely captivated with the fact that I had taught in that school all those many years ago and he showed me around. I felt a wave of nostalgia as I saw my old classroom, now restored to new modernity. He sent for a very old servant who the Colonel felt might remember me. I had my doubts of him recognising me after these many years. He was a gardener in the teacher's house when I was there. The old man appeared in due course, took one look at me and gave me the biggest, toothless smile in the world. Beaming at me he greeted me, with his hand to his forehead 'Salaam missahib' which is an address to an unmarried woman. He remembered me! He said that he took Spotty (my dog) for walks. Certain proof to me that he did remember me but I certainly could not remember him. It was amazing.

The next day we visited Murree and my old school. This trip was the highlight of my holiday. My school was there in all its splendour, red roofed with granite walls and white touches to the woodwork and windows. It was closed because it was February and the school did not open till mid March. It was snowing and the playground was still covered in snow. The *chowkedar* (security guard) would not let us into the building but allowed us into the grounds. I did get a good look at the grounds and the Church.

I will write more about my school, with pictures, following on in this manuscript.

Chapter Nine

Our School days

My dear grandchildren

When I was eight my parents sent me to St Denys High School, an Anglican School for children from fairly affluent backgrounds. It was a private school.

Our school grounds were extensive and were fenced in – to keep the animals out and the children in. But we did have quite close contact with the monkeys as our refectory, or dining hall was adjacent to the fence – almost arms length—and the animals came right up to the fence and we used to feed them through the mesh of the steel fencing. Our dining room also had iron mesh on the windows with about three or four inches open at the bottom. We could just about get our arms through. The females occasionally carried their babies, who were really cute. Feeding them was strictly forbidden by the school authorities but we did it anyway.

We were allowed out of the school under supervision and walked in a 'crocodile' in two's. We loved going into town as our school was high up the mountains, or as we called it 'the hill' at Kashmir Point – the highest point in Murree.

The reason we loved going into town was to see the boys from the Lawrence College wandering about the town. They had more freedom than we did. We also met them, in Church on Sunday. It is a famous old Anglican church called Trinity Church. The boys sat on the opposite side of the aisle. However, we exchanged flirtatious glances with the boys we fancied or who fancied us. It was all innocent fun. Sometimes notes were secretly exchanged as we all wandered out of the church in rows, so that the girls and boys had a brief moment of contact.

Once a month our brothers from the Lawrence College were allowed to visit and those were occasions when we all got together. I remember my brother, Derrick, bringing me his gift – a bit of peanut brittle, wrapped in paper that was very difficult to remove. His meager pocket money had been spent on it and I really loved him for it. We were not indulged with material things as the children of today, but I think we were happier and content with the little we got. We felt indulged, even though by today's standards, our pocket money was like pennies! I still feel we had something that is lacking in today's young society. Our values were very different and totally un-material. I would not have changed my life at that age for the present day.

Derrick and I fought like any siblings at home, but whilst we were in school five miles apart – we loved each other and looked forward to our monthly meetings.

He won the school marathon of ten miles, which was from his school in Ghora Gali (literally translated means 'Horse Valley') to my school at Kashmir Point and back. He was only twelve years at the time. From his school to mine was a steep climb.

Our school was so high up in the mountains that we would look down on the clouds in the valley below. It was awesome looking down on fluffy clouds. In the rainy season the clouds would drift through our classroom windows, covering and obscuring everything until they passed through, leaving us and our teacher damp and chilled. The school teachers were not allowed to close windows. Fresh air was all important.

This is a picture of my school in Murree in the year 2009 that Roger took when he visited Murree.

And this is an old one taken when I was there. Our school was always buried under snow and had to be dug out when we all returned to school after the winter holidays in March. It was just as beautiful in reality as the coloured picture, even though it looks grey and horrid here.

I recall, when we first arrived in England, in 1962, and I worked in London. I was amazed by a comment made by a colleague at work. In the year 1963 it was a cold and snowy winter and she (a director's secretary) said to me,

'You must be thrilled to see snow after coming from a hot country like India'. Pakistan seemed unknown to them.

And I thought, 'can people here in this country where education is so highly rated, be that ignorant about the geography of the world outside of this little Island?' I had already told them I studied in the Himalayan foothills. Didn't they realize we had snow there?

I later discovered that their knowledge of what the Himalayas were and where they were located, was extremely limited.

Today, however, as travel has become more accessible, geography is better known.

Before I went to St Denys, I was in a school in Rawalpindi called the Station School (I visited it when I went back to Pakistan in 2000). It is still there. An incident that I remember from this school was a boy a little older than myself who I have met since on several occasions and who became a Jumbo Jet pilot and flew for Singapore Airlines. On our way home in the school bus he took my English book and scribbled something in it. He was my friend, but a naughty one. I had no idea what he had written but when I got home my father saw it.

In a line of a poem 'Where the bee sucks, there suck I' he had changed the letter s to f. My Dad was furious and stopped us playing with the two brothers. In those days swear words were a heinous crime.

The Station School was a day school. Children with parents, who could afford to, sent their children as boarders to the 'hill' schools to get them out of the heat of the plains and I was sent off to St Denys and my brother, Derrick, to Lawrence College, Ghora Gali, about five miles down hill from St Denys. From the young years to the senior years, we had prep or study sessions (homework here), where the teacher of each subject of the day had set us tasks to do. These answers were then rated and marked. Every Monday morning we had general assembly and these marks were read aloud. They were rated as distinctions, honours, first class, second class etc. down to failure (below 40%). It was daunting, but also a great incentive to study hard and do well. One did not want to look an idiot before one's fellow pupils. It was training for self respect and confidence which was tough on some but a challenge to others.

I loved school and loved to study.

I won't bother describing the school building, because you have the pictures but the grounds were wonderful. Our playground was right down the *khud* side (I am not sure how to translate this word) perhaps hillside would be a good word. The best I can do is to say that it was a decline down the hill with steps cut out of the ground to facilitate walking down to the bottom.

It is here we played all our sports, both with our school mates and inter-school matches of netball, tennis, hockey and a great fun sport called 'dodge-ball'. Of course we had athletics with all the usual track and field events.

We also played interschool sports with Lawrence College Girls' School and the Jesus and Mary Convent, both 'posh' schools for rich parents' children. These games were very competitive. The game we played the most was netball. Each school had two teams, an A team and a B team. These occasions were whole day affairs, with morning breakfast, then the first game with the B teams. Then the hosting school would give the visitors lunch. Each school tried to provide the most lavish meal and so you can imagine what our lunches were like! After this we had time to relax and mix and then it was time for the big game of the A teams. Wonderful times were had by all, with the final jollity of the day – a big tea time celebration and the awarding of the annual trophies.

Above is a snapshot of part of our playground where our plays were performed, in good weather, and where our sports were played. A netball match is in progress.

Every year we performed a classic play or drama and the guests sometime sat on the khud side and watched perhaps one of the Shakespeare plays performed on the playground, or alternatively, they sat on the play ground and watched a play performed on the khud side, which was a wonderful stage-set that had strategically placed trees and natural scenic stage and backdrop. We performed 'Richard II', 'Midsummer Night's Dream', 'Julius Caesar' and 'Robin Hood'. Need I say that this drama queen always had a major role in these plays?

We occasionally spent time with our grandparents, my mothers' parents, in Karachi during our winter holidays where we were spoiled and coddled. My mother's sisters were young and, in my eyes, very pretty.

When I was about eleven I was fretting for my Dad and I played up about going back to boarding school in Murree, so my Mum sent me to my Granny in Karachi who put me in a Convent School as a boarder.

I had no experience of nuns in those days and I remember two or three incidents in this school, but I have no recollection of learning and lessons in any form whatsoever.

On one occasion I was in the bath (a zinc tub – quite big) and was enjoying a cool soak on a hot day, when a nun came in and said,

'Where is your chemise you immodest child?'

'My what'? I asked cheekily.

I knew what a chemise was but I did not associate it with a bath. Why was I supposed to put this thing on whilst in the bath tub? As I was not the meekest of children I spoke up for myself and told the nun that it was the silliest thing I had ever heard. Needless to say, I was punished for being immodest and punished for being rude.

The next day I went down with German measles and was put into quarantine. The beauty was that the quarantine house was on the sea front a couple of minutes from the beach. I loved it, sick or not, and there I remained for four weeks. That is where I first tasted crab curry and it has been a favourite of mine ever since. That is the main thing I remember about that time in the Convent. O yes there was one other incident; the time one of the older nuns died and was 'laid out'. All the pupils had to go and see her. I did not like this one bit. Not only did we have to walk around the bier that she was laid on, we had to touch her and say a prayer. I had never seen a dead person before. I got quite a shock when I did touch the face because she looked fine but was very cold. The idea of a prayer was the last thing on my mind. I could not wait to get out of there.

As soon as Granny came to visit, I told her to take me home or I would run away from the Convent. She was a little bit appalled when I told her my reasons. I was taken home the same day and I think the nuns were glad to see the back of me. Anyway, I was soon returned to the Murree Hills and had recovered somewhat from the loss of my Dad. I decided that St Denys was the best school in the world.

An extraordinary hobby started with a friend and me in St Denys; collecting beetles and caterpillars! This was a mountain town and we had the most marvellous species of beetles. My favourite beetles were the Stag and the Rhino. We had to keep them in secret and it was hard to do this in our school, because the matron and cleaners would inspect everything. We found places outdoors to hide our 'pets', poor things! We also collected the fat green caterpillars, about three to four inches in length and the brown and orange hairy species. We fed them, and I have to say they had voracious appetites. We were hard pushed to keep them provided with green leaves, they devoured everything. We waited for them to turn into chrysalises. We would watch with infinite patience to see the moths and butterflies emerge from these various chrysalises. My friend kept the hairy brown and yellow ones whilst I kept the green, smoothies. They were like velvet to touch. My pride and joy was that one of my chrysalises opened into a most beautiful moon moth with a really wide wing span. I had taken it to my dormitory after the evening inspection by the matron and my friend and I watched it emerge from its chrysalis with the aid of a torch. It was still for awhile while its folded wings dried. It eventually opened its wings, flexed them a bit and flew off into the night. It was beautiful. It seemed to be lit with a pale fluorescent green light.

I suppose thinking back on this memory I should not have been so stern when my little ones, many years later in England, kept racing snails in their bedroom unbeknown to me. I was horrified when I discovered so many of these slimy creatures with numbers on their shells slithering about the bedroom and I made my darling children throw them all away and clean the floor. If I had remembered my youth at that moment and my 'pets' I think I might have been less shocked and more lenient, but one does not always remember things like this at the right time. Now I feel guilty for spoiling their fun – but snails—yukh! Any worse than caterpillars and beetles I wonder now?

School days are the best days as the saying goes and I for one can vouch for that. I loved studying, it was a challenge. For my personality this was what I needed and what I thrived on. I loved anything challenging and did extremely well in school. Besides the study, I had many friends and the boarding school environment was great for companionship and sharing.

My brothers were in the Lawrence College, Ghora Gali. An adventuress tale must be told about my brother Derrick who was about 13 years old. He hated school for whatever reasons boys have to hate boys' schools – and there were many reasons. He decided to run away. He walked from his school, through the mountains, keeping the road in sight but keeping away from roads so no one would find him, and he had some hair-raising encounters with animals. This was wild and uncharted forest. I think he was chased by a camel at one of the villages he went through. He reached Rawalpindi (32 miles away from his school) which is about two to three hours drive on a road with many hair pin and hair-raising bends. He had no money so he walked to Rawalpindi railway station and caught a train to Sialkot, where the family was stationed at that time. The ticket collector asked him for his ticket and decided to let him ride because he looked exhausted and so young. My mother was very shocked to see him and to know what he had endured at such a young age. When he arrived home, he looked thin and emaciated having had no food or liquid to sustain him.

Derrick as a Police Inspector, on his motor bike in Quetta.

Derrick again in Quetta in relaxed mode

Even though he ran away from boarding school, one has to admire his fortitude, determination and courage to do so daring a thing at such a young age.

His education continued in the Boys' Naval College and he excelled in radar and electronics as a trainee. I admire my brother, Derrick, and he and I could talk for hours because his knowledge was boundless. Throughout his life he has been an achiever, not so much materially, but in the seeking and accumulating of knowledge. I remember his dedication in building electronic gadgets in his twenties, when he left the navy. To us, he was magic and could make all these contraptions 'talk'.

When he joined the Police and was made an inspector, he looked very handsome and had the pick of pretty girls. Lorna at the age of not quite sixteen was eventually the one that captured his heart. He was really and truly smitten and was till the day he died (29 November 2008)

It was his spirit of adventure, his daring that made him an achiever and my hero. He was a great police inspector and he and Lorna had a lovely house in Quetta, Baluchistan, where they were stationed and where I spent many a happy time with them. He had a Harley Davidson motor bike that he rode at extremely high speed, like our father. We all loved travelling at speed, except perhaps, Gwen, who likes the slower pace of life. Derrick's and Lorna's garden in Quetta was an Eden of various fruit trees, almond trees and flowers. Quetta was noted for its fruit, in particular its famous mangoes.

I will move on now from school days to my teaching days in Abbottabad, another hill town in the foothills of the Himalayas.

Burn Hall College was a prestigious, elite school for families who could afford its fees. It was a boys' boarding school, but with the kindergarten of mixed gender, day pupils.

My mother, Daisy, was the matron of Burn Hall School in Abbottabad and she was also the nurse, so my family was close to me. Four of my brothers, Mervyn, Raymond, Ralph and Patrick were pupils in school there and I had my own rooms in a large teacher's bungalow when I taught there for about four years, 1950–1954. My elder brother, Derrick and my sister, Gwen (before becoming a nun) came on visits and even though I am informed by Raymond that Mervyn did not finish his final year in Burn Hall, I do recollect him being there. Memories play tricks on us. Since writing this I was informed by Jeanne, Mervyn's wife, that he did indeed do his Senior Cambridge exams in Burn Hall before joining the air force. So my memory is not that bad.

My three Duckworth brothers shared a bedroom in Mum's house and I entered it one day for some reason or the other, which I cannot recall, and was oppressed with the odour of smelly feet. I made such a fuss about it that my young brothers always washed their feet (and socks) before going to bed for years after that. I am sure that they still do. My very real distaste must have made an impression on those three young boys.

As a teacher of the kindergarten class, my pupils were from five to seven years old, therefore a special challenge presented itself as we were unable to communicate as we did not have a common language. My children were day students, not boarders, as our school only took boarders over the age of eleven. They came from affluent Pakistani, mostly Pathan families and were chauffeured or came by coach or even walked with their ayahs to school and back home each day.

The little ones could not speak Urdu or English, leaving me at a distinct disadvantage. Theirs was a dialect called Pushtu. The characteristics of the Pathans included unusually light skin with rosy cheeks and often pale colored eyes and they were astonishingly beautiful children. The little babes, as they were called in school, were terrified at first, but with lots of love and hugs, they soon lost their fear and would kiss me good-morning and goodbye. Tactile communication broke the barriers but communication through language was crucial to their ability to learn, so with perseverance and hard work on their part and mine, the miracle began to take shape.

They eventually learned to read, write and do simple sums. They read English with my accent! I received an award for best teacher of the year for my efforts, and am very proud of it. It was an award usually given to the upper level class teachers. Because of the large number of pupils in the Kindergarten I had two assistant teachers who helped me with the classes though I supervised the lessons for all the little ones of five, six and seven years of age.

The Abbottabad Cantonment area (usually military) had an olden day look, with European style bungalows; various club houses, church and the British Cemetery are still there. The houses are reminiscent of the Swiss style chalets. The old road to Abbottabad from the plains was fairly rigorous to drive on, but now a days it is a bit better but still not ready for the flying coaches that will commute between Rawalpindi-Islamabad and Abbottabad.

Abbottabad always has been a popular summer resort for locals (and tourists) who wish to escape the sweltering heat of the plains.

Spring in Abbottabad and Murree is a magical time. Small clouds play hide and seek in the hills and the air has a nip with frosty mornings and chilly evenings. After weeks of winter rains, that special green of the slopes where spring buds appear, and blossoms are in profusion. It is tranquil and pollution free with many walking routes, and meadows full of wildflowers. To the north is the Black Mountain near Oghi and I am sure it is the one Noel and I tried to visit years later in a company Jeep.

I must tell you about this as it springs to mind. It is not chronological but the mountain is the spur that brings back the memory.

We took our two first children, (Roger two and a half and Lorraine a babe in arms) along with a nanny or *ayah* as she was called, in the back of the Jeep, and Noel and I sat in front. Noel drove. There were no seat belts in those days and we bounced and jostled continuously on the gravelly, winding road. Can you imagine how dangerous that must have been, but we did not even think about that in those pre seat belt days?

After four stressful hours we had only managed to get half way up the mountain and even though we had plenty of supplies, food and milk for the baby, we decided it was a hair-brained scheme after all, and chose to turn around and retrace our route back to the bottom.

Going down was even more frightening than the trip up, with a deep gorge on one side of us and a stony bank on the other. On the steep decline of the narrow road the gravel beneath our wheels made the jeep roll forward, we skidded and slid rakishly downward. The dark of evening was fast approaching so we had to sacrifice a slow and less scary descent for a more reckless one that would get us down the mountain road in daylight. Noel's excellent driving skills saved us from what could have been a disastrous conclusion to this adventure.

I am glad I got this story in before it escaped my memory. Back to Abbottabad now and my story line.

While the entire valley of Abbottabad is breathtaking in its splendor and beauty, there is little to match the spectacular sunrise over snow clad Thandiani, one of the high peaks that is visible from Abbottabad. The snow remains constant through winter and summer and the drive towards the mountain provides lovely views on both sides of the road. The road rises gradually from Abbottabad, passing through picturesque glades as seen below.

This is Nathia Gali en route to Thandiani

In the days of my youth one would come across groups of monkeys along the road but as in Murree, their numbers have now decreased and it would be fairly rare to see them now. I had the chance to travel half way up in an army jeep and found the experience to be exhilarating. It looked as if some of the mountains had been covered with green velvet carpets strewn with wildflowers and rivulets of sparkling water flowing through the crevices.

From a higher zone at night one could see the lights of Abbottabad below quite clearly. To the east the snow-capped mountain ranges of Kashmir can be seen; to the North and North-east, are the mountains of Kohistan and Kaghan, and to the North-west, more snow-capped mountains in the ranges of Swat and Chitral. It's no wonder the 'trekkers' love this area, and a well defined common walking trail has been established from Abbottabad to Thandiani. It's a challenging route to be certain through the thickly wooded countryside with overnight stops along the way. This tourist Mecca, apart from its spectacular views, offers hospitality and amazing generosity from the local hill people. As I can attest, you don't even have to reach the peak (as it is a difficult trek only accomplished by the hardiest few) to experience the outstanding beauty along the route to Thandiani.

A road leading away from Abbottabad showing the town in the valley. The mountains in the background are obscured by mist and cloud, but are visible on a clear day.

Chapter Ten

Your Parents' Very Early Years

My dear grandchildren

Your parents' younger years will be the first branches of the tree that you will want to know about.

I was always very energetic and whilst I was pregnant, I never let up on my dancing and living it up as it were. Noel and I were party goers and I didn't miss a chance to have fun. We had many friends. The only thing that was different when I was pregnant was that I could not stand smoking or the smell of it, even though it was 'cool' in those days to smoke and I did smoke normally. I did not have any cravings and things like that either. I just took pregnancy in my stride and never let it interfere with my life style.

My first baby, Roger, was born in Lahore on the 16th May 1955 in the United Christian American hospital. A beautiful baby boy who filled me with joy (as did all my children the moment I set eyes on them). He was delivered by an American male gynecologist. I had all the latest available facilities of the time and bringing my son into the world was easy. He was born at around 8 pm and weighed in at 5 lb 12 ounces. Even though he was tiny he was perfect and beautiful and by the time I was returned to my private ward it was about 9.30 pm. I slept fitfully because of my elation and excitement and I was given my son, whose cot was in my room by my insistence, in the early hours of the morning. I insisted on doing everything for him and tired myself out. I became very tearful because I was exhausted. The doctor ordered that Roger and cot were removed from my room. He was put in the nursery with the other babies.

I was given a sedative, or something that put me to sleep, until I was fit again to be a mother without dissolving into tears, which was a few days later. Hospital confinement was not like today. Then they kept mothers and babes in for about two weeks.

We lived at that time in a roof terraced flat of a three storey house in Temple Road, Lahore. My parents-in-law, lived in one part, my sister-in-law and brother-in-law, Joan and Derek, and their three girls, Nanette, Janet and Maryanne, lived in the main part. Hence we were a family within a family which was quite the norm in Eastern homes. We shared for convenience, to be together and for economic purposes. It was great and made for a wonderful togetherness and a close family relationship. This closeness made a strong bond of family ties and has stayed like that until today.

Noel's and my flat consisted of a large bedroom, a very large open walled terrace, and a WC. The lounge and dining room was common to the family as was the bath and shower rooms downstairs. As Noel was away a lot in the Sind desert, Roger and I shared the bedroom in winter. There was room for a double bed, wardrobes, dressing table and Roger's cot and paraphernalia but we slept under the stars on the terrace in spring and summer, with mosquito nets and huge pedestal fans in the summer months.

No insects could withstand the force of those pedestal fans, but I was never about to take chances of mosquitoes biting my son. He was encased in a secure mosquito net in his cot. As my family increased, more beds were added to the terrace and sometimes the other kids, Joan's children, also came up to our terrace to be cooler. We had a lot of fun in those far off happy, carefree days.

In spring we had the kite festival of *Basant* (I think it means coming of spring but I am not sure). Our terrace was a great place to fly kites from – it was a roof top terrace as were some of our nearer neighbours and every roof top in Lahore had ardent kite fighters – it was called kite cutting. The *manja* or string that was used (enormous reels of it) was glued and steeped in grounded glass to enable the cutting of an opponent's kite string high above in the sky. There was a knack of cutting that Noel was adept at – it was to do with the angle you pulled your kite across the opponent's *manja*. If you can imagine a reel of thread magnified about fifty to a hundred times, with a rod through the middle hole of the reel to grip and so the thread could flow freely, then you have a *danga* of *manja*. Well, Joan and I would be holding the reel while Noel and Derek, and any guests that were over at the time, were flying the kites. However, we all had a go at flying and cutting. By the way at this time all the kids would be asleep, preferably in the bedroom downstairs, with ceiling fans on full power and with their ayahs in attendance.

Kite flying and cutting was exciting and skillful. One particular night we were partying late and suddenly I felt something on me – it was trailing *manja*. I grabbed it (something one did not do, because of the glass). It had a heavy tug, so Noel took it over. I remember it very clearly. He had protective gloves and gradually pulled this kite down. It was a slow procedure, because if you pulled too hard the manja would break. Everything about kite flying needed skill. Noel's easy, unhurried, hand over hand pulling gradually paid off.

It was dark and we could not see the kite but we knew it was big, really big by the pull on the string. Suddenly this huge – five foot across – *thookal* (not sure of the spelling)—a special kind of kite, shaped differently to the normal square, hovered over our heads while we all gazed up at it in amazement. It was enormous and in perfect condition and it was our prize. I will never forget the excitement of that night. It was only made of paper, but one would imagine that we had been awarded a huge prize of value. We were ecstatic!

The rich people tied money to their kites, sometimes high value notes. Hence the chasing of kites had a double incentive. If anyone saw a floating kite – other kites were truly being controlled and one could tell the difference. There would be a general shout of '*bowkatta*' and the kite would be watched and then chased by many children and adults. It was really a mad thing when I think on it now, but it was such good fun and I was well and truly a fan and a partaker of this sport as were thousands of others. All the roof tops in Lahore were crowded and there were several accidents too with people falling off in excitement of catching a cut kite's string.

In July we had the monsoon winds and torrential rain. May and June were hot and dry so when the monsoon rains came; it was a relief and a blessing to all. The children would strip to their underwear and stay out in the rain. It seemed to cure prickly heat which was a curse to all of us in the really hot months. The temperatures would reach nearly 100oF. I hated the heat and stayed out of it as much as I could.

The worst weather torment imaginable was the dust storm. The dust permeated every crevice no matter how much the servants tried to keep it out of the house. They would make sure every door and window was closed and they would put padding where ever there was a chance of the dust coming in. No matter what one did, the dust would creep into the house and cover everything. We would see the black cloud on the distant horizon and at times, in the middle of the day, our world would go black when the dust cloud covered the sun and was directly over us. Invariably there would be a power cut and all the fans would stop. The wind would howl and hurtle dust particles, like tiny shards of glass at any unfortunate person out in it. At first the wind would be hot, but as the storm continued and the wind howled, the air would gradually become cooler. As suddenly as the dust storm arrived, it would depart and the rain would pelt down furiously. It least we knew the rain would follow the dust storms but to endure them was most unpleasant.

Another form of pestilence that occurred was the locust storm. Again one would see this dark cloud approaching over the horizon and wonder what was due to cover us. It was nothing like rain clouds, but ominously black. Suddenly we would hear a whirring sound approaching. It is hard to describe, because it was frightening to hear. We would all run for the house and close every door and window. Each locust was about 2-3 inches in length; they would cover every tree and everything green and edible. They remained for an hour or so and then they would depart en masse. We would hear this flutter of millions of wings taking off and they were gone with a few crippled and wounded left behind. Every tree and piece of green foliage would be devoured, leaving our lovely green garden city denuded of its beauty.

And once again, the rain would follow and within about two weeks all would be green again.

In the winter months, Lahore would get very cold. There was not snow, but every little puddle would freeze. My children would join their cousins in their large rooms downstairs. It sounds horrendous in these modern, western times, but it was just lovely and we all have great memories of those days. We would all sit around together and there would be story telling and singing together. The rooms were large and had lots of windows and ceiling fans. What's more the children had a great deal of fun together.

It is difficult to describe the joy of sleeping under the stars on our terrace in the summer time, high up above the city's hustle and bustle. When Noel was home, he taught me all about astronomy and I knew all the constellations in that visible hemisphere. He learned most of this from my brother Derrick. We both loved the same things, Noel and I. He loved poetry, like me, and composed many for me and wrote others that were funny. I wish I had kept all. I have one that he wrote when he was just nineteen. Many things were lost when his case was stolen in the Sahara desert somewhere or that he lost on his travels. One of my grandchildren has a similar trait of losing things! No need to mention names here.

When Noel and I were apart, which was a great deal of time, we wrote daily letters to each other for the twenty three years of our marriage. These too I had right up to the time I married Terry – they filled a case. To accommodate my new life, I reluctantly destroyed those two years after my marriage to Terry and now I wish I had not. They were love letters so perhaps it is a good thing that they are not about for others to read. I remember them. All my letters to him came back with his belongings after he died and even those I destroyed without ever reading them again. It would have been too painful. A love story of thirty three years – but it is locked safe in my memory.

I have one letter that missed being destroyed and one that I was writing when my son brought me the news of his Dad's death. Both of these I keep in my letter treasure box.

Backwards to happy times. The full moon at night was bright enough to read by. On darker nights the Milky Way curved across the midnight blue sky, lighting it up with billions of silvery stars and some pulsars. We saw many shooting stars, flying across the heavens, some with lovely trails of light. It was common in India to say that if you saw a shooting star you could make a wish – a little bit of nonsense but it was fun. These starry nights were beautiful. As Noel and I always went out dancing till the early hours, we saw these starlit skies on many an occasion when we came home to our beds under them.

Well my darlings the above is an introduction to your Granddad Noel. How I wish that you had known him and that he had known you.

Roger was a lovely baby, but for the first three months of his life, he drove me crazy with constant crying at night. All day he was adorable, smiled at everyone and slept a lot. He was cute, chubby (not fat) and it turned out that he cried at night because he was hungry and needed a supplementary bottle. Problem solved but in those days, keeping a bottle warm in winter was all right but to keep one cool enough in summer was a problem – we had no kitchen on the terrace. And so it was kept in a wide mouthed flask. One improvised in that non-technological age.

I will recount a story about Roger when he was about two and we moved to Karachi. I was pregnant for Lorraine and Noel wanted us to live in Karachi which would be nearer to where he worked in the Sind Desert.

There are two purposes for this little tale – one because it is about my son, but the second is to give you a picture of the great Railways left by the Raj and the luxury of travelling on a train in those days of plenty. I am writing now about fifty odd years ago.

Train travel in those days, unlike today, was quite luxurious, reminiscent of the days of the Raj. The distances were long in mileage and in time.

We had a first class carriage all to ourselves – five sleeping berths all leather or may be just leather look. The compartment was air conditioned and the windows were large with tinted glass to protect against the glare. In those days we travelled with bedding rolls, with leather straps. The beds were made up beforehand inside the bedroll which when opened was shaped like a cross. The head and foot of the roll had cases, where you slipped in the pillows, after the thin mattress and sheets were made up and a cover was laid across the two 'arm' sections. The arm sections were then folded to make the bed roll into a long rectangular shape. It was rolled up and secured with leather straps and buckles. All one had to do was to undo the straps and roll it out on the berths and, voila, one had one's bed!

These hold-alls were quite ingenious and had plenty of space. They were light because they were made of rain proofed canvas and they were used by everyone in the days of the Raj and beyond – that is anyone using the railway. Journeys went into two or three days as Pakistan is a big country.

Well, we were happy to have a five berth compartment all to ourselves – not many could afford to travel first class in those days. Just before we set off, a man boarded and so we had a travel companion. He was smartly dressed and respectable. He smiled at Roger. Roger glared back at him as if to say 'how dare you come in here?' The man turned out to be some kind of professional and was very taken with my unfriendly son. He settled himself on the opposite side of the carriage, occupying an upper berth to give us more privacy.

Being a Muslim he would say his prayers at regular intervals during waking hours of course. Roger watched him in fascination and eventually decided to imitate his gestures, much to my embarrassment. Our companion was amused and chastised me for trying to restrict Roger's imitation. As our long journey progressed, my son and his new friend prayed together several times a day. We eventually had our meals together. Roger decided to accept him with grace.

The catering service on the North Western Railway, was a firm called Spencers. The bearers (servers) wore white uniforms with white fan tailed turbans, decorated with green bands with the Spencer logo on the front in green and gold. They wore green and gold cummerbunds. Their uniforms were very impressive as anyone living in those days will remember.

When the train stopped at a station (timed to suit meal times of course) the waiters would come aboard and take orders with an *a la carte* menu. At the next stop meals were served on silver trays with china crockery with the Spencer logo on everything. It was very posh and the food excellent. The train took off and food was enjoyed by the travelers; the used trays were collected at the next stop. The first two stops were timed about half an hour or so, the eating session stop took much longer; well over an hour or two. In India and Pakistan distances between towns are extensive.

Another memorable story of Roger in Karachi. We were at friends' home when he decided to have a crying fit over something he wanted and I wouldn't let him have. He held his breath, as babies do; went blue and limp and then passed out. I was terrified.

Ailsa and Eugene Pellier, our friends grabbed him from me and tried everything. She was a nurse and I thought she knew what to do. However, he went into a coma and she thought there was no heart beat and he had stopped breathing. Talk about a mother's instinct! I gave him artificial respiration through the mouth and then pumped his lungs; I also gave him a teaspoonful of brandy! I think I prayed and bribed God more than my treatments (which I had only learned as a girl guide). However, he eventually choked on the brandy and started breathing, but did not recover consciousness. Ailsa, who was a non-Catholic brought her husband's Sacred Heart cloth medallion and put it on Roger's chest; confident that it would work.

Eugene had already called a doctor, who came and threw us all out of the room. Not sure what he did but I heard Roger cry and the doctor called me in. I was totally traumatized. The doctor told me that I should never let my baby get in that state of frenzy again as if it was my fault. If he held his breath, I was to tap him gently on his cheek or leg to make him breathe straight away. (I wonder what the modern world would say today to that doctor's advice.)

When Lorraine was due to be born in the Holy Family Hospital in Karachi – by my calculations this was still a few days away—Mervyn, who was stationed in Mauripur, decided that he was taking Noel and I out to the Blue Lagoon Night Club, about one and half hours' drive from where we lived. My Mum looked after Roger. Heavily pregnant, I wore the most beautiful white silk maternity suit. It looked stunning – not sure that I did but the suit certainly did. I was not very big anyway.

The Club was enchanting, with a lagoon and lots of fairy lights draped in the trees and a band dressed in white linen suits. I sat there, tapping my feet to the beat music, but drew the line at rock-n-roll at nine months. I did, however, dance to the slow numbers. At midnight I started getting twinges of pain and I was timing them before alerting my two escorts because I knew they would panic. I did, however, tell them as the pains became regular and then there was panic – not me – the men! I was calm and knew I had time to get to the hospital before the birth, but having to cope with two panicky men was worse than any pain I was enduring!

Inevitably by the time we got to the hospital and I was examined, the pains stopped and I was, embarrassingly, sent home and told that it was a false alarm. This was now nearing 2 am. At 3 am the pains were back in earnest and Merv had left to return to his base in Mauripur and so Noel had to find a taxi on the deserted streets. We eventually got to the hospital, which was near to where we lived. He was furious with the nuns who had sent me home in the first place.

And so my Lorraine was born in the Holy Family Hospital in Karachi on the 11th June 1957 at 5 am and weighed 6 pounds 6 ounces. She was a pretty little doll.

Noel was present, but not allowed in the delivery room because the nuns did not agree with men getting in the way of delivering babies. They, the nuns, were cold, efficient and just got on with the job or made me get on with the job. Give me a sympathetic man any time! I have to admit though, it was the quickest delivery ever; in at 3.20 am and Lorraine was born at 5 am. The Nuns should not have sent me home in the first instance.

That night I dreamt that Mervyn had a plane crash and was hurt. I woke up in a state of distress, but soon realised it was only a dream and then forgot all about it. I wanted my baby with me, but the nuns had rules that nothing could change.

Mervyn came to see me in the evening with Noel. I had a shock when I saw Merv, because he looked a mess – scratches and bruises on his face and I was very upset. He told us he had problems and had to bail out of his aircraft. His parachute ballooned and he was dragged for miles in high winds. Anyway he was scratched all over, but nothing serious, he just looked a mess.

With the two men cooing over this beautiful little doll child, I felt quite superfluous and unimportant. It got to the stage where I wanted them to go and leave my baby with me. The nuns would not give me time with her – they kept taking her away from me because they said I needed rest. They were probably being practical but I felt deprived and was glad to get home and have my little girl all to myself.

Unlike, Roger, she was not demanding and was instead a placid and good natured baby; a total joy to me. No breath holding with this child, however she had a pair of lungs that could let rip when she wanted something.

By now we were living with my mother who was the housekeeper to some millionaire in Karachi. She had her own house, within the grounds of the mansion. The house was expansive, and Mum thought as she had such a large house, we should live with her because Noel worked away from home most of the time and Mum could help me with the children even though I had an ayah.

My memory is a bit foggy here as memory of long ago days is inclined to be unreliable at times, but I do seem to remember Mum and no one else – perhaps my siblings were in boarding school and my Dad away somewhere. By this time I should think my siblings were working and Gwen was either in the convent or training to become a nun. Derrick was in Quetta. However, Mum, is uppermost in my memory for this part of my life in Karachi and also the millionaires (whose names escape me). They wanted to adopt my son and 'give him much more than I ever could'. Crazy people! She could not have children and wanted my boy – what a hope! These rich people seem to think they can buy anything if they have money.

Noel was back in the Sind desert at the time. I packed my bags, boarded a train with my babes and returned to Lahore and safety. Back to our really inadequate by now rooftop flat. As Lorraine was born in June, we slept outdoors. I had an ayah for the babies (so that Noel and I could socialise when he was home). We loved going dining, wining and dancing and did so nearly every night. I didn't work and Noel was on holiday. I had Mother Green (Noel's Mum), Joan (who was ever ready to have my babes who she doted on and spoiled) and the ayah to take over the night time shift, but most of the time the children were asleep while we were out; usually from 10 pm till 2 or 3 am.

I decided to work for a while and attained a job with an American company in Gulberg, as Executive secretary to the CEO. I was picked up by the company chauffeur driven car at 6.30 am, taken to work for 7 am until 2 pm, when I was driven home again; a complete working day. The chauffeur driven car was a privilege offered to executive secretaries.

After lunch, we all slept until about 5.30 or 6 pm. We then showered and the kids went out with the ayah for their daily walk to the beautiful Lawrence Gardens when the weather cooled down a bit and where all the ayahs met and the children played in safety.

When Lorraine was about one and a bit, I fell pregnant for Diane. I continued working, dancing and having fun until the eighth month. We had a hail storm in January, with hail stones the size of marbles. They covered our terrace completely. We were downstairs in the lounge and I needed to go upstairs to the terrace flat for something or the other. I was warned to be careful.

As it happened, the minute I stepped onto the terrace I skid on the hail stones, desperately trying to stay upright, I fell forward on my stomach. I didn't seem hurt, but I was afraid that my baby might be. For the life of me, I could not get up as the hail stones were rolling about and I could not get a foot-hold. After shouting for help, Noel came up and pulled me up, the pair of us slipping and sliding. I was well and truly told off for my recklessness.

I went to the hospital for a check up to see if my baby was safe. She was fine I was told and seemed to be moving and kicking as usual and so I began to relax.

Diane was born, perfect and unharmed, in the famous Sir Ganga Ram hospital, Lahore at 8 pm and weighted 6 pounds 12 ounces, on the 6th February 1959 with her Aunty Joan in constant attendance in the delivery room, telling the midwives and doctors what to do and what not to do. Very embarrassing for me.

The night before Diane's birth, Noel had arranged to go on a wild boar hunt. He wanted to call it off – just in case she was born the following night. By all my calculations, she was not expected for a couple more days and so I convinced him to go off with his friends. The next morning he came home and found I was not at home and so he 'flew' to the hospital after a sleepless night of wild boar hunting and blamed me for sending him hunting.

He was delighted with his baby girl as was I. She was a treasure then and still is, with her father's wit and her father's bad habits; very much an Elston-Green. When she was home, her Aunty Joan took over. She considered Diane her baby because she saw her enter the world and that was enough. All this spoiling made Diane I am sure, a breath holder. She got the treatment of a smack when she did this, but Joan would take her from me and run away and protect her. However, she never did what Roger did even though she was a little tyrant for holding her breath. I was terrified of breath holding and still am to this day.

Noel was working on the Mangla Dam, the largest man made dam in the world at that time, and he was employed by another American company. We moved into a village called Dina and lived in a very large brick house in the village. We were the only English speaking people there. There was so much space in the house (and the countryside) that we really spread out and had more room than we had ever had.

Noel and I loved to wander about the countryside and we became known in the little village. We were often invited into the villagers' huts and given a glass of milk, as was the custom which I drank with relish, but Noel would not. It is a Muslim custom to feed anyone who entered into a home and it was considered bad manners to refuse their hospitality. One felt bad because of their poverty, but it was not good to refuse either and so we ate with them of their meager fair. Simple but delicious.

We were there for almost two years when Noel was offered another drilling contract in the Sind again and so we moved back to our little home under the stars, crushed and cramped for a while but we were soon to have the whole house to ourselves.

Mum and Pop Green, Joan, Derek and the kids all left for England. I was expecting Caryl at the time and decided to stay on for a year or so. We still had a terrace on the top landing to use if we wanted to sleep out doors, but Noel had installed thick cuss-cuss tatti chicks in the downstairs rooms. Cuss-cuss is a type of grass that is woven together to make these chicks. He invented a drainage system to have constant water flowing through them. On the inside of the chicks were pedestal fans, blowing cold air into the house. Not only did it cool the house, but the smell of the cuss-cuss was wonderful. I think we had one over on the air conditioning of today, because it was healthier, cheaper, no noise and it had a lovely smell.

Having so much space had its draw backs. We had to buy furniture to fill the rooms even though a few pieces had been left for us. We had a roaring wood fire in the lounge in the winter which was a great delight to all of us and we spent many a happy time together playing with the children, listening to music and playing games. What we would call today, quality family time. There was no television, just the radio for news and music – we were in touch with the latest, without the visuals. For that we had the cinemas.

Two years later Caryl entered the world with enough confusion as is her wont. She was born in the Railway Hospital, Lahore on the 15th January 1961 at 6 pm and weighed 6 lbs 10 ozs, more than Diane.

At 3 am I developed contractions which seemed pretty regular and since we had no car and there were no *Tongas*, (horse drawn carriages) available at that time of the night, the only available transport was our neighbor's motor bike! Luckily it was large Harley Davidson and the pillion seat was one I was used to sitting on as my brother had the same bike and so off we went to the hospital. Like Lorraine, the contractions disappeared after arrival. Another embarrassment. Home again on the Harley. At 3 pm of the same day the contractions started and this time I was sure.

Caryl arrived, delivered by my friend who was the attending doctor. I always wanted a child with dimples. Well at last my Caryl was born sucking her thumb, with dimples and all. A total joy and a beautiful baby.

Therefore all my children were born in Pakistan. Pakistan came into being in 1947. I could not help but impress upon them as they grew up, although they only lived there for a very short time, my pride and affection for their birthplace because that was where their roots existed in the vast subcontinent.

The children had a lovely life there as did Noel and I. We were comfortable and lived well. By now we had several servants. We had a Cook, a bearer, two ayahs, a *bisti* (water carrier) to water the garden and fill our bath sink/pool for the children to play in, a sweeper who cleaned the floors and the bathroom, a *dhobi* (laundryman) and last a young man to play with Roger. He was known as the ayah's assistant and his name was Peter. Peter was about seventeen. Being young he was full of mischief and would tease Roger by singing to him 'Beautiful Brown Eyes'. For some reason this infuriated my son. He would whine and create a great fuss. Peter would be chastised by the ayah. He was a lovely little lad and was a help to the cook and the bearer and made his services to the other servants indispensable.

I taught my children later in life to look on Pakistan as the land of their birth, and to be proud of the fact, for the very short time that they lived there and, hopefully, you too will treasure that something that makes you that little bit different and special.

The children when they went to the gardens for the evening walks would collect fireflies in a bottle and bring them home. It was sad that I had to make the children let them out. I explained how cruel it was, even though they looked so pretty twinkling like many Tinker Bells in the clear glass jar. The children seemed to get the message because they would open the jars and let them out themselves. Those fire flies were a delight in the bushes at night, like so many fairy lights twinkling away amid the night scented Jasmine bushes.

Anyway it was soon time to move on as it was rumoured on the grapevine that the educational system was to have English taught as a second language. We did not want that for our children and so we decided to leave for England (which was my choice). Noel wanted to go to Australia or Canada but my reasoning was that he was always away from home in some desert or the other so I should have the choice of a country to live in. He agreed and so England was our next home, but that is another part of this manuscript. The English adventure will follow in a later chapter because there is much more to tell about India and Pakistan.

Whilst still in Pakistan, Roger and Lorraine went to school. Both when they were five. Diane was three when we left for UK and Caryl just eighteen months. Only their early years were spent there. Roger remembers quite a bit (he was seven when he left) and Lorraine remembers a few things about her school. Diane and Caryl have no recollection at all of the country of their birth.

Both Roger and Lorraine went to private schools in Lahore.

On leaving Lahore, we had to give up everything including money, furniture and our dog 'Buster' a German shepherd. Luckily, my Mum took Buster over and cared for him and when she left for England, he was adopted by an Army Colonel. And so our sojourn in Pakistan came to an end. With the children carrying new gifts, bought at Karim Baksh, one of the larger stores in Lahore. Caryl had a cuddly toy, Diane and Lorraine something similar, but Roger wanted a banjo. I had instructed them to choose something small. We tried to dissuade Roger, but he was determined to have it. I told him it was his responsibility on the journey because we were travelling by air and it would be inconvenient. His heart was set on this banjo and he and it could not be parted. He left Pakistan with it and arrived in England with it. During our stop over in Karachi it was with difficulty that he parted with it to sleep; he wanted to take it to bed in the hotel in Karachi and sleep with it. On the plane the next morning there was the same trouble with the Stewardess offering to put the banjo in the lockers. He became so upset that she allowed him to keep it under the seat in front for take off.

The children were good on that journey but they were well spoiled with toys and attention. I knew one of the cabin crew girls and she was very taken with Caryl. Lorraine and Diane loved the experience of flying though Caryl cried at take off and landing. Probably because her ears hurt.

'Adversity opens the mind and the pen writes black' – Helen Renaux

Chapter Eleven

A Concise History of India and Pakistan

My dear Grandchildren

Let me start this chapter with a little history lesson and make use of the subject I learned in school, Indian History, which I hope will entertain and enlighten you with knowledge of India.

Firstly, and because this is our heritage, I will commence with the Colonisation of India by the Europeans. The French, the Dutch, and the Portuguese – not necessarily in that order, but fairly close, invaded India under the guise of trading and finally the British did the same thing. The French and British fought many battles for possession of territories in India. The French held the South and the British the Northern territories. After many skirmishes, eventually the British, with the aid of Robert Clive of the East India Company in 1751, with 200 British and 300 Indian soldiers, helped defeat the French. Britain eventually gained rule of the sub-continent of India and the British Raj was born (the word 'Raj' being translated to English means 'reign') in the late 1700's.

These Europeans are surely our antecedents, whether they like to admit it or not, because they are responsible for our existence and what we are today. Obviously they could not resist the beautiful Indian women and between the rulers and the ruled, they produced mixed children who, as it happened, turned out to be a truly beautiful mixed race.

If you read, and I recommend that you do, William Dalrymple's book 'White Mughals' 2002, which is a popular history pertaining to just one such intermarrying affair during the time of British colonialism. The affair saw a British dignitary convert to Islam and marry a woman of royal Mughul descent. Dalrymple's work, complete with the analysis of sources, has won acclaim both as a work of literary and historical merit, which may give you an example of the sort of beginnings that took place to form the Anglo-Indians as we came to be known. As you probably know that 'Anglo' means British and Indian is as it is, but our family for one is not strictly Anglo-Indian, because we have French, Portuguese, English and Indian blood in our genes.

The British colonised India as an emergence of the 'Industrial Revolution' in the west, during the nineteenth century, which started in Britain and spread to other regions of the world, where industry was depleting the use of manpower. Britain desired to invade and conquer other lands because they decided they had a right, because of their invincible naval and military forces, to invade and colonise other countries. India was just one of those countries.

India was fictionally and factually known as the 'Jewel in the Crown'. Factually because of one of the many jewels Britain 'appropriated' whilst ruling India, the famous 'Mountain of Light' being the Koh-i-Noor Diamond which now adorns a Royal Crown in the Tower of London. The diamond now weighs 108 carats, whereas when it was owned by a famous Sikh Emperor, Ranjit Singh, it weighed 240 carats. There is much speculation as to where the rest of the diamond disappeared. Apparently, it is rumoured that the famous owner of the Koh-in-Noor, left it to his son, Duleep. Duleep was a child of eleven when he inherited his father's title and all of his riches, including the Koh-i-Noor. This son, supposedly, gave it to Queen Victoria as a gift. Allegedly, this gift to the British Queen was improbable, because the new Emperor was only a child and had no authority to give away a jewel of such value that its worth could feed the entire population of the world for a few days. Below is an excerpt I found whilst researching the diamond, which might be of interest to any reader of this manuscript.

'According to some sources, the Koh-i-noor diamond was found in the Godavari River in central India 4,000 years ago. Tradition associated with it, a state that its owner will rule the world, but that to possess it is dangerous for any but a woman. This may have been a delicate piece of flattery to Queen Victoria, who once owned the gem, bequeathed to her as a gift by the child Sikh Emperor.

The 'authentic' history of this jewel begins in the 14c when it was reported to be in the possession of the rajas of Malwa. It later fell into the hands of Baber, who founded the Moghul dynasty in 1526. During the next two centuries the diamond was one of the most prized items in the treasury of the Mogul empire.

In 1839, Nadir Shah of Persia invaded India and all of the treasures of the Moghuls fell into his hands except the great diamond. Nadir Shah was told by one of the emperor's harem women that the stone was hidden in the Indian emperor's turban. The conqueror then invited the conquered to a feast and offered to exchange turbans as a gesture of friendship. The emperor had no choice but to agree. Nadir Shah, later in the privacy of his tent was known to exclaim, 'Kohinoor—Mountain of Light' when he discovered the diamond and so the stone remained in the possession of the Persian dynasty, although many attempts were made to regain ownership of it. The Persian king was assassinated, and his son Shah Rukh, was deposed. In an effort to discover the whereabouts of the diamond Shah Rukh's eyes were put out, and boiling pitch was poured on his head, but he refused steadfastly to reveal its hiding place. Later, a Persian king fled with it to the Sikh Court in India, and Ranjit Singh, known as the Lion of the Punjab, took the stone and wore it as a decoration. It was later placed in the Lahore treasury. After the Sikh wars, it was taken by the

East India Company as part of the indemnity levied in 1849, and was subsequently presented to Queen Victoria at a sparkling levee marking the company's 250th anniversary.

This is one story. There are however many tales about the Kohinoor Diamond. One more likely to be true is that Duleep Singh, the eleven year old son of Ranjit Singh, inherited the Kohinoor, with most of his father's wealth and the title of Maharajah. Duleep was influenced by the British and became quite anglicized. Because he was a child he was easily influenced and manipulated and it is alleged that the Kohinoor diamond was gifted to Queen Victoria by Duleep because he was so besotted with her Majesty taking such an interest in him. Duleep was sent to England at an early age and requested that he convert to Christianity. He spent his life in England, living in a mansion called Elverden. There is a book about him, entitled 'The Maharajah's Box'. It is very interesting and historical. If you are interested in British/Indian history (as I am) it is a good read. The famous Kohinoor Diamond is synonymous with Duleep Singh. My daughter, Lorraine was my introduction to this book. However, she found it too historical and less romantic (it is a romantic story but it is historical romance) whereas I wanted the history and less of the romance! The choice of one's reading is all to do with individuality and individual taste.

Below are some statistics and details of the famous Kohinoor Diamond, which has always been of interest to me. Not because of its worth, but because of the morality in its acquisition by the British and the deprivation of India of its enormous value.

Weight: 108.93 carats
Cut: round brilliant cut diamond

The Kohinoor diamond was displayed at the Great Exhibition of 1851 where it was thought to display insufficient fire. It was decided to re-cut it from its original Indian form, and a member of the Amsterdam firm of Costar was called to London to cut the stone. A steam-driven cutting wheel was set up, and Prince Albert set the stone on the wheel, while the Duke of Wellington started the cutting wheel. The cutting took 38 days, but did not add much more to the stone's brilliance. It was believed that the historical value of the diamond was diminished by the cutting. Queen Victoria continued to wear it as an ornament, and then left it to Queen Alexandra, who wore it at Edward VII´s coronation. In 1911, the jewel was used in a crown made for Queen Mary, and in 1937, in another made to be worn by Queen Elizabeth at the coronation of her husband, King George VI in 1937. The Queen Mother's crown with the Koh-i-noor is now in the Tower of London.'

Because this diamond has always fascinated me, I went to the Tower to look at the Crown Jewels and expected to see something really spectacular, but it was just a very big diamond. I think it must have been its romantic history that fascinated me more than the actual jewel itself.

India's wealth was beyond belief. The Aga Khan, in the days long before partition, was alleged to be weighed in a scale with uncut diamonds and other precious stones and the funds raised through the sale of these diamonds and jewels was distributed amongst the poor of his territories. Wealth in India was not very evenly distributed it is true, just as today but he was a prince and it would appear, a generous one with his people. However, one has to admit it was India's wealth, its spices, its minerals, including gold, diamonds and other priceless gemstones and the vast country itself that helped to create the Great British Empire. Therefore, it could be acknowledged both factually and metaphorically that India was the 'Jewel in Britain's Crown'.

Queen Victoria's statue in bronze graced the plaza, at Charing Cross, The Mall, Lahore, in front of the Assembly Hall in all its glory, in Lahore. This memorial was crowned and named 'Victoria Gloriana—Empress of India'. I don't have a picture to show you of this Queenly statue. I will put together many pictures and bits of historic excerpts to add visual dimension to this manuscript.

This statue is supposedly now is Lahore's fabulous Museum. This building is in Victorian architecture, designed by a British architect but built by Indian craftsman in Mughul dome style, as are most of the Victorian buildings in India. There are many throughout India and Pakistan. They are beautifully, and some would say, elaborately carved, but in keeping with the exoticism of the East, and more or less built in Gothic architecture with Mughul type domes and some with minarets, they are truly a mixture of architectural styles. One has to admit that they are well maintained – especially as they are in the path of the Monsoon winds and rains which take their toll of these great Victorian structures of art.

Below is all I could research on the famous sculptures that made an impression on all who saw them in the days of the Raj and since. I will leave Miriam Qureshi to take the pen to give you information.

'Now you see them, now you don't . . . '

By Miriam Qureshi

LAHORE: As you stroll past the Punjab University old campus on The Mall, you cannot miss the sole bronze statue of a man that stands on the sidewalk. The inscription below the statue reads: "Alfred Woolner (1878-1936), a great and beloved leader."

Alfred Woolner was the vice chancellor of the Punjab University from 1928 to 1936. His is the only statue left of many that were positioned in front of prominent buildings during the British Raj in a wave of imperialistic civic zeal. Now, with the title of 'colony' no longer hanging over our heads, we are in a better position to appreciate the aesthetic value and historical importance of these effigies. That is if it's not too late.

"The statues were a significant part of my youth," said Sajjid Abbas, a septuagenarian Lahori who knows the city like the back of his hand. "I would often walk down The Mall and take photographs of these beautiful sculptures because I knew that they would disappear one day." There were a total of ten such statues, each narrating the grandeur and the might of British rule, said Mr. Abbas, taking a walk down memory lane and relating the history of each of the sculptures. The first on Mr. Abbas's list of these "emblems of British authority" is the bronze statue of Queen Victoria that was placed in the pavilion of the assembly chambers.

"Her Majesty would stand there cradling the scepter and holding an orb, dressed in her long imperial gown with a veil of hornito lace covering her face," said Mr. Abbas. "The statue was removed from Charring Cross in September 1951 and taken to the Lahore Museum but the marble pavilion remains, displaying a bronze replica of the Holy Quran." The queen's statue was cast in 1900 in London by B MacKennal and the grand marble pavilion, with its Oriental design in stark contrast with the anglicized statue, was designed by Bhai Ram Singh Mistri, the deputy principal of the Mayo School of Arts.

"At the Lahore Museum, one could see Queen Victoria's statue with the busts of her sons, George V and Edward VII, displayed alongside," said Mr. Abbas. "There was also a full figure statue of King Edward VII, riding a horse, which used to be displayed near King Edward Medical College."

However, the most significant and controversial of these statues was that of Lord John Lawrence, who was viceroy (1864-69) and also served as the governor general of Punjab. The statue, placed in a small garden near the Punjab High Court, displayed the following inscription: "By which will ye be governed: by the pen or the sword?" In the 1920 protests against the British, many nationalists objected to the offensive caption.'

Below is one of these buildings – the Lahore Museum, situated in Lahore, Pakistan where Queen Victoria's statue used to abide, perhaps still does today. The Queen's statue was very beautiful and majestic however the pavilion that housed it was even more beautiful and was built in white marble. It is still there today but the pavilion now holds a pedestal with a copy of the Koran in a glass case. The other picture is part of a large park in Lahore where my children's *ayahs* took them in the evenings for exercise and fresh air, in those days called 'The Lawrence Gardens', now named 'Jinnah Bagh' after the Qaid-i-Azam, the founder of Pakistan.

The British were superb architects and engineers, with the help of the Indian natives. As mentioned earlier they were responsible for the Railways, the Telegraph system and the picturesque Indian Police Force. They built fabulous buildings. They made India technically a very prosperous country for the British but one has to admit that all benefited from the British enterprise in India, long after they left in 1947.

Below is an excerpt from the internet but it is well written and I feel it is good to add here. It is here because I have an affinity for this particular city. I was there during the bloodletting days of partition and was witness to much horror and terror. It is also where we lived before coming to UK.

'Lahore being in the middle of the Punjab,—a region now split between Pakistan and India— was on the frontlines of the bloodletting that accompanied the creation of Pakistan in 1947. The city was gutted by communal rioting and by the flight of Hindus and Sikhs to India who, before partition, lived side by side with its Muslim population and Muslims fleeing from India and crossing the border into Pakistan.

Now, the winds of peace with India are fanning the embers of a renaissance that began in the 1990s under Nawaz Sharif, the Lahori former prime minister. The city is sprucing itself up for a growing flow of visitors from Delhi and other nations—many of whom have memories or relatives there – with a fancy new airport, refurbished colonial buildings and ambitious hotel projects, some that border on the luxurious. The roads are smooth and wide and the whole ambiance of the city is attractive.'

I visited St Anthony's Boys School in the year 2000 and 2006 which Roger attended from the ages of five to seven, and where three of my brothers schooled. We stayed with the school Principal, Group Captain Cecil Chaudhry, now retired from the Air Force. I also visited the Jesus & Mary Convent – where my five year old Lorraine went to school. I must say that on my return to Lahore in 2000, I was amazed and duly impressed with its modernity. With temperatures hovering around 46c, Lahore is best left well alone during the mid-summer months. However, even in the summer the city is at its best in the evening, when the sun slips behind the rooftops of the old city and tints the great marble domes of the 17th century Badshahi Mosque a fiery pink.

Because India was a wealthy country this could be seen as a good reason for Britain to conquer it and to, in their way of looking at it, help India to become civilised and to bring together the three main separate cultures (Hindus, Sikhs and Muslims). That was the stated policy. However, and more likely, the conquerors gained a great deal of wealth and power for their little worlds in Europe. Babur to Shah Jahan and his son Aurangzeb, who was the last of the Moghuls to rule, comprised the Mughul dynasty. Babur was a descendant of Ghengis Khan and Tamarlane (or Timurlane), but more familiarly known as 'Timur'. The Moghuls were of Persian, Turk and Mongol origins. Shah Jahan was the great architect who built the Taj Mahal as a tomb for his beloved wife, Mumtaz Mahal, just one of the many memorials and forts built during his reign.

Below is the Taj in sunset:

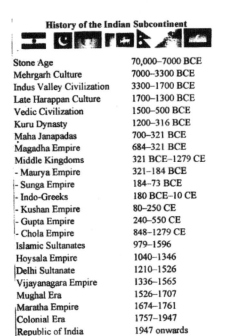

History of the Indian Subcontinent

Stone Age	70,000–7000 BCE
Mehrgarh Culture	7000–3300 BCE
Indus Valley Civilization	3300–1700 BCE
Late Harappan Culture	1700–1300 BCE
Vedic Civilization	1500–500 BCE
Kuru Dynasty	1200–316 BCE
Maha Janapadas	700–321 BCE
Magadha Empire	684–321 BCE
Middle Kingdoms	321 BCE–1279 CE
- Maurya Empire	321–184 BCE
- Sunga Empire	184–73 BCE
- Indo-Greeks	180 BCE–10 CE
- Kushan Empire	80–250 CE
- Gupta Empire	240–550 CE
- Chola Empire	848–1279 CE
Islamic Sultanates	979–1596
Hoysala Empire	1040–1346
Delhi Sultanate	1210–1526
Vijayanagara Empire	1336–1565
Mughal Era	1526–1707
Maratha Empire	1674–1761
Colonial Era	1757–1947
Republic of India	1947 onwards

Above is a cutting of the history of Indian cultures and civilisations.

To help make this reading even more historic, perhaps I should take you back much further than I have so far in my narrative, to the first invaders of Northern India, the Aryans in 1,500 B.C. It is known that the Indians of the North are fair skinned, as are many of the Pathans and others; some with blue eyes and light hair because of this initial invasion. However, like our history, there was inevitable intermarriage with the Indians and now they are just lighter skinned, but many still maintain their light eyes and light hair. I know this for a fact because when I taught in Burn Hall, Abbottabad, in the Himalayan foothills, I came in contact and taught many Pathan children.

For centuries, the sub-continent of India, with its beautiful Himalayan mountain ranges, the Hindu Kush and the Karakorams, its forests and vales, its rivers and plains, has been coveted and invaded by Greeks (Alexander the Great for one), Russians, Persians, Turks, Mongols, French, Dutch, Portuguese and the British. They all wanted this beautiful fertile land and have all fought each other for possession of various parts of the subcontinent of India.

Pakistan in later years constructed and is now in possession of the 'Karakoram Highway', the old 'Silk Route' that was the route used by traders. Now it connects Pakistan to China as described below:

"The present highway is also popularly called the 'Silk Route' by many romantics because it approximates the trail of what was once one of the many silk, jade and spice carrying caravan trails that congregated somewhere near Xi'an, in China, and terminated in the vicinity of modern Syria on the Mediterranean sea coast. Like long lines of exploring ants, determined traders, merchants, and adventurers wore a path through narrow gorges, high grass sheathed valleys,

across waterless deserts, around 6,000 meters – and higher mountains, and over raging rivers in pursuit of barter.

The passing of time has not altered any of these geophysical conditions, nor were the reasons for building this new road (apart from its obvious military significance) any different from the ancient reasons for undertaking such a hazardous journey. The new road was built to facilitate trade between China and Pakistan." (Travel book by David Leatham)."

This is just a little background history of this exotic land of mine and your parents' birth. India and Pakistan still have the occasional skirmish, or war, yet India has many Muslims living there and Pakistan is home to a few Hindu families.

I was amazed when I visited Mumbai (Bombay) for the first time in 2001; at its cosmopolitan cultural integration. The population of Mumbai appears to celebrate each cultural feast and festival. At Christmas time Hindu's, Sikh's, Parsi's, Muslim's and Christian's houses are illuminated with lights as are all the shopping malls. At Diwali (one of the many Indian festivals) all cultures celebrate with chirags and candle lit decorations. Diwali is one of the prettiest festivals with lights all over the city. It is also the noisiest! And at Holi (another popular Hindu festival) everyone joins in the celebration by covering themselves in coloured tinted water. At Eid (a Muslim feast) as many as possible of all religions visit the famous Haji Ali mosque that juts out to the sea. The walk way to the Mosque is cut off by the tide in the evening, leaving this lovely white building seemingly floating in the sea.

I stayed in Bombay in 1944 for about two weeks as an Air Force officer cadet when it was under the British Raj during the Second World War and, reluctantly, I have to admit that it was a very beautiful city then. Marine Drive, with the famous Queen's Necklace, so named because of the lights, visible from the sea, circling the bay was a wonderful sight. There was not too much traffic congestion in those days and with many nightclubs, night life was very active. The beaches were clean and one could swim in the sea.

Having said this, however, I still feel an affinity with Mumbai and love it the way it is today as I did in 1944. Mumbai's teeming population has its own type of charisma.

It would seem that the people of India and Pakistan are friendly but it is the politicians of both countries seem to have enmity. One of the main problems of their dispute is the beautiful Vale of Kashmir, part in Pakistan but some parts; the beauty spots of Jammu and Shrinagar are in India. The population is mostly Muslim, but the ruler is Indian. When the British were in India and discussions about the division of the countries took place, the subcontinent was divided in a way that would seem to be strange to say the least, with Pakistan being partly in the West of the subcontinent, divided by India and then another strip called 'East Pakistan' (now an independent country called Bangladesh) in the East. The country of India was dividing these two areas of the country of Pakistan.

I hope that this romantic, exotic, though traumatic, history lesson may be of interest to you or anyone who comes from, or whose ancestors came from this great land of wealth, beauty and opportunity, as it was in those long gone days before all the plundering, destroying and conquering took place.

According to William Dalrymple, there are many families in Europe today who, if they traced their lineage far enough back to the Raj, would discover that they shared both ancestry and even a blood line with India!

I, personally, treasure my past experiences in that wonderful India where I was born. I feel privileged to have had the experiences of my life out there. For thirty five wonderful years I lived in India, schooled in the foothills of the Himalayan Mountains in an elitist school, St Denys High School, taught in one of the most prestigious boys' schools, Burn Hall, in Abbottabad, again in the Himalayan foothills, worked in India and Pakistan, married there, and had my children there and I would not exchange a single day of my experiences – even the horrors of partition remain a part of my life in India.

My children came to this country when they were very young and hardly know anything of their heritage and ancestry except, perhaps, the stories that I have told them. However, I feel that as I am in my 85th year, it is time that our history is recorded for posterity or else it will be lost forever.

Not many of my generation still exist, or can recall, great moments of history that affected our family. Such as the world historic event of the dividing of a subcontinent into two separate countries, India and Pakistan, which took place in 1947, and the havoc, death toll and chaos that this historical event caused to the two nations and to those living there at the time; our family for instance. We lived on the very border of the two countries involved – a few miles apart and so we experienced all the horror of Partition in its full force and destruction.

I do not think that I will ever be able to write much of this in graphic detail, it was too horrific and over the years, I have sub-consciously eroded it from my mind, but I will tell what ever I can consciously remembered later in its chronological place.

Any man's death diminishes me, because I am involved in Mankind; and therefore never send to know for whom the bell tolls; it tolls for thee.

—John Donne, 1624

Chapter Twelve

From There to Here—East meets West

My darling Grandchildren

We had a wonderful life style and did not really wish to leave Pakistan and go through this big upheaval, but it was necessary, or so we felt, for the development and well being of our children. We decided to emigrate and join the rest of our extended family who lived in England. However this decision meant leaving my mother and father, my young brothers and my sister in Pakistan and our dog. To me this was a big heartbreak.

Our main reason for leaving was because of seemingly valid rumours that education was going to be taught in the vernacular (Urdu) as a first language and English as a second in all schools. As our mother tongue was English and we all learned with English as a first language in school. This rumour to us was a major upheaval where education was concerned. Leaving the country seemed to be the only option we had if our children were to benefit educationally. Like all the many post colonials; most of who had left after 1947 and through to the 1950's, we too now decided to 'go home' in 1962. Home, but where was home? Noel wanted to go to Australia or Canada, but I wanted only England because I had been indoctrinated by my upbringing and heritage to feel inclined towards it, and so it was to England that our departure was targeted. Let me say here, that this move was not something that I personally relished. I did not really consider England my home. My home was where I was in Lahore, Pakistan and before partition, the subcontinent was my home. I have never to this day been able to totally break the ties that bind me to the Orient but now, after 49 years, England is my second and loved home.

However, to continue . . . Noel loved the sun and heat because he was accustomed to living in a desert environment through his work as a driller, but I hated the heat and could not wait to live in a cool country. This desire for cool weather made my departure a little less painful.

We had to contend with the immigration laws of the UK. We had to prove our right to enter there. Parents', grandparents' documents were vetted and after many weeks of waiting, we were approved by the British High Commission as accepted immigrants to England but they could not give us passports, only entry permits. This coincided with Enoch Powell's 'war' against immigrants storming England's shores and airports.

We had to obtain Pakistani passports and visas – all very stressful and tiring as Noel was back in the desert and I had to do most of the chores of moving to another country.

Our banks had to be cleared and in addition our home contents had to be disposed of. Most of our home contents had to be given away as there was no such thing as small advertisements in newspapers as they have in UK. No one in countries like Pakistan and India are interested in buying second hand items. As for money – that was a joke. All we were allowed to bring into UK was the tiny sum of £10 per person, in our case £60 in total to start a new life in a new country with a foreign culture to the one we were used to! It seemed ridiculous but it was a ploy to keep immigrants out of UK and Pakistan's desire to keep Sterling in their Country.

We managed to buy GB pounds at an exorbitant rate on the black market, but even this was limited and considered breaking the British law. The Pakistan black market was thriving and they did not care how much one bought in GB pounds. We were afraid – it was a risk and we had to hide the money somewhere in the bed rolls and hope that it was not discovered.

Spending surplus money believe it or not was a problem. We went to expensive restaurants, took the children to a super store to choose presents or keepsakes for them to take on the journey. We stressed that they had to be small enough to take on an aircraft. Lorraine and Diane chose sensible things, but Roger decided he wanted a banjo. We did all we could to dissuade him, but his heart was set and so with misgiving we allowed him to have his banjo.

We bought first class tickets to use yet more money and we had to travel from Lahore to Karachi, stay overnight in a hotel near the airport and fly out to London the next morning.

Saying goodbye to my Mum and my servants, all who came to the airport to see us off was heart rending. The children's ayah was crying and wailing, 'How can you take my babies away from me?' It was true, they became very attached to each other and all her crying was distressing the children, the girls any way. Roger was too interested in the aircraft and his banjo. He did not like saying goodbye to his Nan. Unlike today our send off party at Lahore was standing fairly near the aircraft that we had to board, making the departure even more traumatic when we did board. My heart was breaking saying goodbye to my mother. To see her standing there with a courageous face, trying hard not to let me see her pain was terrible because I knew she was feeling as bad as I was. I must have given her a hundred kisses and said goodbye countless times before actually boarding the aircraft.

Noel was busy consoling me and I was trying to sort the children out. Fortunately they were more concerned about the aircraft and all the fuss the cabin crew were making of them. They were fully occupied and their minds not concerned so much with goodbyes – more full of wonder and excitement.

The aircraft was an old Dakota, unpressurised because it did not fly at high altitudes like jets. It was comfortable enough but the children suffered ear pain on take off and landing. I did too for that matter. However it was an adventure and we were willing to put up with any inconvenience.

In Karachi the children were tired but excited to be on an adventure journey. We allowed them to run around the hotel lobby to help burn up some energy before supper and bed time. We had a job to get them settled at the hotel for the night. We were due for an early morning take off from Karachi airport.

They did eventually drop off to sleep, cradling their special toys. Roger kept hold of his banjo which I tried to pry loose as he slept – all to no avail he grabbed on to it, seemingly still asleep. I gave up.

Early the next morning there was chaos. Collecting and dressing the kids, getting the luggage through check out. Luckily there was a flight attendant who I knew as we boarded the Boeing 729, one of the most modern of the year 1962. As we were the first to board as First Class passengers, we were seated and all was well organized as the children settled into their seats with toys and activity kits, provided by the airline to amuse them. Roger showed no interest in these and just clung to his banjo.

On take off the stewardess had to take it away for storage and he was most distressed. When the aircraft was in flight his banjo was returned to him. He held on to it even when he was asleep we could not release it from his grip.

The flight attendant took Caryl off my hands and had her in the galley with the others stewards, so I was able to spend time amusing Lorraine and Diane with their drawing and painting. Noel had Roger seated next to him. It was a pleasant and uneventful journey. We stopped in Tehran, Persia the now Iran, Zurich because in those days the aircraft had smaller fuel tanks and needed refuelling. We had to disembark in Zurich where the rest area was spotless and very comfortable. It gave the children time to run around and expend some pent up energy which was good.

We stopped yet again in Frankfurt to allow passengers on and off the aircraft.

At last we were on the last leg of our journey.

We eventually started our descent into London Heathrow. The time was 6 pm and it was still bright enough to see the landscape. Looking down at London as the aircraft banked it appeared green and picturesque, with doll's houses and tiny handkerchief size gardens. Everything seemed in miniature to us as we were used to big houses with acreage, but London looked beautiful. The greenness was what impressed me the most. I fell in love with the country and knew I had chosen right.

We were to be met by Derek and Joan and at last we touched down at London Heathrow. Everything seemed fine until we went to collect baggage. As Noel removed our bedrolls and cases from the carousel, our luggage evoked peculiar looks from other passengers and airport staff, as if we were bringing in strange objects. The bed rolls were a source of amusement to everyone and a source of embarrassment to us. We had no idea why they were causing so much amusement. Bedrolls were the norm in British India and in the divided countries after partition, they were strong, practical and had amazing storage capacity so why all this mirth over bedrolls? Obviously they were a novelty in London airport.

Going through Customs as foreigners was another ordeal – our light brown faces didn't seem to matter but the bedrolls were certainly a curiosity. We were asked to open one up as the customs were intrigued with this peculiar type of luggage. All that could be discovered were quilts, bed linen and clothes. We held our breaths about the cash stored in one of them somewhere. However, it was not discovered. The bedrolls caused much attention—in the way they opened, the pockets they contained, the efficiency and the lightness of the canvas seemed of interest to one and all.

The children were becoming restless and Noel and I were getting a bit irritated with the attention paid to these nondescript baggage containers. The Customs seemed more interested in our bedrolls than in us.

After much confusion and curiosity, we eventually were through Customs and were met by Derek and Joan. Suddenly more problems with the bedrolls, how and where do we fit them into the car? Even though they were light, they were bulky. We eventually had to get three taxis for the luggage and ourselves as we all could not fit in one car; the problem was solved. We drove along the London streets to get to Kent where we were to settle, being ever amazed at, to us, the tiny houses. Tiny in comparison to the spaciousness we were used to in Pakistan.

At last we arrived at Derek and Joan's home, which was soon to be ours as they were buying a house in Bexleyheath. Their present apartment was in Erith, Kent. It was a maisonette, with three bedrooms, two fairly large and one smaller, a large lounge/diner, a hall, kitchen and bathroom. The maisonette contained lots of windows giving the rooms plenty of light—in fact it was quite a sizeable apartment. However, it was a bit cramped as Joan and Derek had three girls, Nanette, Janet and Maryanne, older than my children. We had all lived together in Pakistan, in a much bigger house no doubt with three floors, so this cramping was not too unendurable as it was only for a few weeks or so we thought. We were just happy to be together again.

We talked and laughed till the early hours of the morning. The children had been put to bed with the usual bed time stories.

Noel and I had a bedroom with Caryl in her cot, the five girls (three of Joan's and two of mine) shared a bedroom with two sets of bunk beds and one single bed in one of the bedrooms, and Joan and Derek shared a room with Roger. We were a bit cramped but quite comfortable as the rooms were adequate. The lounge too was large and just being together again after our sad farewell in Pakistan was a very happy time for all of us.

Over crowding the West would call it but to us it was cosy and companionable. With our Eastern heritage, a family staying together was the norm. We loved the togetherness.

My children had not ever done anything in the way of fending for themselves and when they saw Joan and Derek's three girls vacuuming and dusting, my little three year old, Diane, asked her Aunty,

'Aunty Joanna, do you want me to do the 'jhar ponch' (dusting)'?

This amused all of us. Only Lorraine had picked up a smidgen of Urdu in Pakistan, but none of the others had, so we were surprised to hear this from Diane. She must have heard her ayah say the word, but I had never heard her use an Urdu word before. It sounded so cute from this tiny person.

The radiogram was on and they were playing the Bachelors singing 'My Diane'. Diane listened for a bit and then said, 'How do they know my name?' She was at a really cute stage of development.

The next important thing to do was to arrange the children's schooling. We had to find schools for Roger and Lorraine. We discovered they could not go to the same school. As we were Catholics, we wanted them to go to Catholic schools because we felt they would get the best education in those schools. All arrangements were made and the first day they were escorted to school. The girls and boys schools were separate. Lorraine settled into her school well. As she was five she was fairly new to school life anyway. She had spent only a term in her Convent school in Pakistan and the change over to England did not seem to disturb her much. Roger, however, went off to school full of enthusiasm but on his return home, he said with total disgust

'This school is no good. I have done all the work in my school in Pakistan and they are not teaching me anything new.' I went to see the teacher and he explained that Roger was a bit advanced in his learning skills, but he said he would gradually fall level with the other boys. I was not too happy about this, but there did not seem to be anything I could do. I did not want Roger to become blasé about learning in this school. In time he settled and all went smoothly.

Noel and I had agreed on this schooling together. We had discussed private schools for the children but there were none close by and I was not able to drive then—at least I had no license to drive in UK. I wanted my children near me and not in boarding schools.

Noel soon received an offer of a drilling job with an American oil company in Libya. He wanted me to come with him as they had offers for family living in Malta. If I agreed to go, I would only see him at weekends or once every two weeks. I thought it a daft idea with the children only recently settled in school. I did not want my children in boarding schools in England whilst I traipsed around the world with Noel.

Luckily Joan and family had not yet moved out to their new home, though the move was imminent. I was a bit nervous being left on my own in this new country without servants and four children. We had no furniture and the maisonette had three bedrooms, a lounge diner and kitchen to be furnished and equipped.

The year after we arrived, 1963, was one of the coldest winters experienced for many years. There was no central heating in the maisonette but we had gas fires.

Everything was new and strange. I had never had to cook and work in a home. My servants did all that. I had never used a vacuum cleaner and certainly viewed a toilet brush with suspicion. I was a total green horn in this domestic lark.

Joan allowed me about a week to get the feel of living in UK, before she handed me a chicken and said, 'cut it up, babe, I am going to teach you to cook'. I glared at this funny thing with distaste and said, 'what is it?' 'It is a chicken'.

'But it has no feathers. If it is dead I will not touch it'.

Chickens to me ran around pecking in the earth and had feathers. We did not have supermarkets nor did we visit butchers' shops. That sort of thing was done by our cook. If by some accident on trips out and about, I saw a shop with meat, I would look the other way. It sickened me.

Joan said to me, 'Either you learn to forget the East and learn how to do things that are necessary here, or your children will starve. You have chosen this life, now get on with it. There are no servants here to do your bidding. You have to do everything for yourself.'

Scary instructions from my loving sister in law, but I guess it was true! I did not have a clue what to do to joint that piece of flesh and so she showed me how to. She did a bit and then passed it on to me.

I found it distasteful to say the least but I did it and she showed me how to cook a chicken casserole. And so began my new life in UK. Noel had already left for Libya and his drilling contract. Joan and Derek were due to move into their new home soon and I would be left with an almost empty house, four children to get to school, and housework. There were still a couple of weeks to go before Joan and the girls left. At least while Joan's girls were around, they took my girls to school. Roger's school was very close and I walked there with him for a few days and then he decided he could go by himself.

The day of Joan and Derek's departure arrived and the chaos of moving ensued, with the children getting in the way of things. To say it was stressful is putting it mildly. I was devastated because I knew I was going to be on my own with four children under eight. Where were my ayahs, my bearer and my cook? How could I possibly manage? I could honestly say I was terrified at the prospect, but then I was always adventurous and I told myself this was an adventure; something new; a challenge and so I attacked it full on.

I had Noel's contract letter with salary and allowances, which in those days was really good. He was paid in US dollars and his monthly salary went into a Jersey bank. I opened a bank account in Erith, Kent where we lived. It was Grindlays and with the GB£ at really good value, the transfer of dollars into my UK bank account was great.

Joan had left me her cooker and washing machine; a kitchen table and chairs. She had left me some mattresses and bedding on loan. I had to get carpeting, beds, lounge furniture, utensils, crockery, cutlery and just about everything a home required.

I went to the Cooperative Society with Noel's contract letter. Joan had told me about Hire Purchase. I had no credit rating as I was a fairly new comer to the country. However, when the hypermarket saw how much I needed to buy, they accepted my story and Noel's contract and gave me everything I wanted.

In a matter of days my goods arrived. First the carpets arrived. It was the sixties and so the carpet for the lounge was patterned but the furniture was plain black leather. I had ordered a centre table, a radiogram and television for the children. I loved music and the kids loved watching children's television in the evenings. These were our luxuries.

The carpets for the rest of the house were beige. There was no central heating, but there was a gas fire in the lounge. I bought two electric heaters for upstairs and horror of horrors; we put an oil heater in the hall downstairs. Many people had them in those days so at the time it seemed fine and safe. Luckily for us we had no problems with it. It had a large globe of mesh that used to get red hot. The heat it exuded warmed the whole house. It was amazing, but today it would be considered extremely dangerous. It was all encased in a safety cage so it was fairly safe.

Not many people had telephones in their homes at that time, but Noel insisted that I have one installed so that he could contact me. It turned out a real God send.

When all the furniture and furnishings were in place, it was quite a cosy home and I began to settle in. My cooking left a lot to be desire, but I learned how to cook simple meals, that the children liked. I took the two girls to school on the bus and Caryl and I returned home. She was nearly two years old, but quite a good child.

Life seemed so hectic; there was no time for socialising as I was used to doing in Pakistan. I shopped for food and cooked food and then fed the children. It seemed to be all about food.

In this country it seemed as if my life consisted of cooking food; washing clothes; cleaning the house; taking the girls to school or collecting them. Roger took himself to school and returned on his own.

What had I let myself in for in this new life I had chosen? I still hated handling meat but I had no choice but to do so. I learned and learned quickly. I missed my bearer and my cook but most of all I missed my ayahs.

There was always the television for the children after school while they had their snacks and I got their dinner ready. I could not get into this habit of having 'tea' at about 7 pm. At home (Pakistan) we had dinner at 8 pm.

However in the '60's in Pakistan there was no television but the children were always occupied in doing creative things and amusing themselves with their ayahs in constant attendance and I was always there for them in the lives.

Their very young life schedule in Pakistan was waking at 6.30—7 am with morning milk and biscuits on the terrace. They found the newspaper; at that time the big newspaper was *The Pakistan Times*, and they would fight about who would 'read' the paper first. It was something that made them feel important! Roger was the only one who could read a few words – he was four. They got washed and dressed, which was seen to by their ayahs. See an example of the children's chota *hazri (*small breakfast*)* which was their milk and biscuits below!

Every picture tells a story – the girls got to the paper first and the look on Roger's face tells all!

Soon after their breakfast their ayahs took them for a walk to the Lawrence Gardens where they had wonderful areas to play and be supervised. After their lunch, about noon, they would have an afternoon nap. Their ayahs slept too. The rooms were darkened with blackout blinds and the ceiling fans put on. They also went to the gardens after afternoon tea—4 pm. They showered and changed and went off to the Gardens at about 5.30 and retuned at 6.30 pm. If Noel and I were not going out, the ayahs would go off for a couple of hours. All meals were provided for our servants by us, except when they went off duty. They then preferred to have their own cooking.

And so the years went by; the children grew. Roger and Lorraine went off to their private schools and I got rid of one ayah. There is more about our children's life in Pakistan in a chapter dedicated to them. This is just a comparison to the life in Pakistan and the big change in England. The children became accustomed to the change very quickly but it took some time for me to adapt.

The children were seldom ill in Pakistan, but not long after being in UK, they got every contagious disease that one can imagine. Measles, chicken pox, whooping cough, German measles and then there were the colds and flu type viruses and Caryl constantly had tonsillitis – it was manic for me. I did not know what hit me! Luckily for me, I had registered with a doctor just across the road. He came to the house as I had two at a time, sometimes three, down with something or the other. The main thing is even though all of this was traumatic for me, I managed to cope somehow. I suppose when the time comes one does what one has to do. But it was tough.

I learned all right but I had to learn the hard way. The first year was the worst but gradually things settled down and life continued in a fairly normal way. I longed for Noel's holiday time; two weeks in every eight weeks; so not bad at all. When he was home, he hired a car and we drove all over England. We had day trips or visited relatives and friends for weekends or a couple of days away. We took the children to most of the sights in London and various castles.

Lorraine was amazing with her sense of direction. We never found out how she remembered the way. She got a real kick out of the beauty of England. One day she startled Noel and I by suddenly saying, 'Oh look Mummy, Friesian Heifers'. I did not have a clue what she was talking about; only later to discover they were a breed of cattle. She was only five but probably learnt about them in school. No wonder she studied biology for her 'A' levels!

Our first year in England was difficult to put it mildly, but we all coped. Illnesses were taken in hand and dealt with; I managed to cook quite adequately and bought myself some cookery books. I did, however, miss socialising. I missed dancing and night clubbing as that was such a big deal in our lives in Pakistan. I was thirty six and very young for my age.

In October 1963, my Mum came to live with us temporarily. It was wonderful to have her with me in England. She stayed with us for almost a year. She took over most of the housekeeping and set me free from total domesticity! I got myself a job in Erith with a firm called 'Submarine Cables' as PA to the CEO. It was great to get back to work. Certainly different to my jobs in Pakistan where I was picked up from my home by a company chauffeur in a company limo! Here I had to walk to work and back every day; another cultural shock.

At least when Noel came home, the two of us went out quite a bit as we had Mum to baby sit. She loved it and so did we. She missed our children when we left Pakistan. Their Elston-Green grandparents lived with Joan and Derek and they met from time to time.

My Mum left eventually for her own place in Teddington in Surrey with my brothers.

I had to leave my job and get back to being a full time mother and domestic chores. I really enjoyed this new type of freedom from outside work and put my heart into looking after my children. The high pressure had gone and I was quite adept at my role now.

Joan never did get on with our mutual in-laws and the inevitable happened; a big row and Mum and Pop Elston-Green decided to leave them and asked if they could come live with me. I sincerely and happily welcomed them into our home. They were my God Parents (as I converted to Catholicism when I was nineteen). I loved them and so did our children. Noel was happy too.

And so began my life with my in-laws and a happy one it was. Mum was a great cook and a very loving grandmother to my children, and Pop was a real live angel in every way. He took the children to school and picked them up in the afternoon; made their porridge every morning when he made his own. He polished their shoes every night and put them outside their bedroom doors for school in the morning. I think my children had the most highly polished shoes than any other pupil in their respective schools. I told him not to do it and that I could handle that job, but he would not give up his self appointed task.

Mum told me to get a job if I wanted and I did. I went to work in London. I travelled from Erith to Cannon Street and then did two underground journeys to get to work in Clerkenwell Road. It took nearly two hours each way, so I was travelling for four hours in a day and doing a nine to five job. At first I came home exhausted but in time I got used to it and it became a normal everyday task.

My work was interesting. I was PA to the Advertising Director of a Technical Magazine. I had my own office which is something that I always seemed to have in my various jobs.

I used to wear stiletto heels and I have to say that in the snow, they were totally incorrect. I had a fall on my walk to the office from the tube. I did not get hurt, but getting up in the icy snow was not easy. I eventually had about six guys around me offering help. I was very embarrassed and managed to get to my feet on my own. I eventually condescended to boots, which I thought, were ugly and heavy looking for my type of dressing or in the summer low heeled pumps.

I wore mini skirts and tights with my boots – always the trendy chick me. My boots had to be sleek with heels; none of those sensible low heel shoes for me.

I cannot say that my children were deprived in any way by me working. Their grandparents gave them a great deal of love and attention. I came home at seven in the evening, and I gave them baths and read to them. This was a pleasure for all of us. We were a family of readers. It was a real incentive for bed time. Roger read his own books but the girls, Lorraine and Diane enjoyed me reading to them, Caryl enjoyed listening for a while and because she was younger, she soon fell asleep.

I so loved this time with my children; all of us cuddled together in my bed (when Noel was away). When he was home we took turns in reading to them. This lovely time did not last long as the years went slipping by and the girls soon read their own books.

I remember coming home from work one day and walking home from the station, I saw Poppy walking with Lorraine. As soon as we got close I saw the state of her face. I screamed and was in a state of panic, when my little daughter, with her face all bloody and swollen, was more concerned about me! 'It's fine Mummy, it doesn't hurt. Don't cry Mummy, I am ok.' Some mother I was when my injured daughter had to console me. I could not come to terms with my children getting hurt or ill. Actually she had hurt her mouth and displaced her front teeth.

All I could think of was how much it must be hurting her and that it was going to disfigure my beautiful little girl.

I took her to the dentist the next morning and he said that her teeth would steady themselves as they were still baby teeth ant that the swelling would subside. There was no major damage. She did not start losing her baby teeth till she was eight.

Roger passed his 11+ exams and was accepted by St Joseph's Academy, a prestigious school in Blackheath. He was taught by the De la Salle brothers. When Lorraine was ten, she too passed her 11+ exams and went to Erith Grammar School, leaving Diane and Caryl still in St Fidelis in Abbeywood.

My four darlings, Riverside at Erith, Kent 1963

Caryl and Diane snapped in their school uniform. Caryl was five and Diane seven.

It is man that can make the Way great, and not the Way that can make man great.

Confucius

Chapter Thirteen

Your Grandparents – Noel and Norma

My dear Grandchildren

I have to say a little about your granddad, Noel and me here, the parents of you parents,

I didn't want marriage – life was too full for me. I was busy having fun with many friends both male and female and I certainly did not want children. However, your Granddad Noel had other ideas and was a very persistent suitor. We met officially at a tea dance (or jam session) as we called them, which were common in those days. They were held in the afternoon in big hotels or night clubs (about 5 pm) with a live band and dancing and lots of alcohol or tea if you preferred. My friend introduced us because she was married to Noel's brother and she knew I loved dancing. When she said he was the best dancer, I was ready to meet him. I always loved to dance. It was customary in those days of good manners and etiquette that the boy approached a girl and asked her to dance politely. I pretended not to look, but I did watch surreptitiously as he swaggered across the floor and approached me.

'Hi, want to dance?' I expected something more like, 'May I have the pleasure of this dance.' Oh well I danced and he was heaven to dance with. When the tea dance was over about 10pm, we went off together to have dinner in one of the many night clubs in Lahore, then danced the night away till the early dawn.

That was the start of a ten year romance that included every emotion that existed within it. Noel, I learned later had seen me riding my bike past his house for a long time and had every intention of making my acquaintance.

Well the night was great and I discovered he was in demand by other girls; always a lady's man! As time went on we were together a lot, and even though I was not ready for any commitment he would not take no for an answer, besides he demolished every other man who had any interest in me (and there were many) or even innocents who just looked at me. He was a terror in that respect; a fighter, who wanted me for himself, but apart from this he was the most affable, charming and popular person you could meet. He was popular with both women and men. His had a great personality with a dry, cryptic sense of humour, the best dancer, tough and masculine and hence popular with the females. Because he was so tough he was therefore respected by men.

My brother Derrick and Neville Hine were his best friends and could tell you a tale or two about him. They were very close.

In brief I married him for two reasons – first I loved him more than any other man, because I respected him for his love, his loyalty and his sheer power of personality. The other reason I married him was because he would not allow another man near me for any length of time. His persistent and constant pursuit wore me down. He was a boxer who was selected for the world Olympics, but broke his arm just before the time. Basically my parents disapproved of Noel because of his boxing, hell raising and drinking but to me he was a real fun person to be with.

I tried meeting others to please or pacify my parents and also to try to defeat this forceful man who was pursuing me with such persistent intent. I got engaged six times; all to no avail. He got rid of all the fiancées, systematically, in his own dogmatic way. Some stood up to him and tried to fight for their rights, but he conquered eventually. All this took place over a period of ten years. He just would not give me up. How could I not be impressed? There is so much more I could write about him – it would fill this document and leave room for nothing else. Suffice to say that he was an amazing man, this father of my children. We had a tumultuous and exciting life together but never, ever boring.

At the end of our ten year courtship, what really woke me up was to see him at a New Year's Eve ball with a very pretty woman. I went with my latest and last fiancé, who was tall, blue-eyed and very good looking with a professional position in work and totally approved of by my parents.

Noel and his lady friend had a table in this very plush hall, complete with crystal chandeliers, a sprung dance floor and a forty piece orchestra. There was a balcony running all round the hall. Noel was watching us and I was aware of it; nervous at what he would do. He invited Peter (fiancé at the time) and me to join them as we did not have a table. Everything went well and I was beginning to relax, though I did not like Noel being with this other girl. However, when they played the midnight dance, Noel ignored his date, grabbed my hand without saying a word. I had no option but to acquiesce and we danced the 'midnight ball' dance together. This dance said a lot; one danced the midnight dance at the ball with one's true love. The other two in our party were left to themselves. Immediately the dance was over, he returned to the table; left me in the middle of the floor; collected my bag, saying nothing to our companions and then escorted me to the cloak room, ordered our coats and we left. He proposed for the hundredth time on the way home and I eventually said 'yes'. I was not about to take any more chances!

I woke my sister Gwen and told her the news. She was ecstatic, as she always loved Noel and felt he was meant for me.

Eventually we were married in St Anthony's Church, Empress Road, Lahore on the 20th June 1954, with Derrick giving me away, Mervyn in attendance as our witness, Gwen as one of my bridesmaids and Jeanne (Lesley Anne's Mother) the other, and the two little flower girls, Nanette and Janette, Joan's daughters. My parents did not attend my wedding, but Noel's parents did. It was a happy yet sad day for me, because my Mum was not there. It was also the hottest day of the year. I will never forget how hot it was – 100oF.

We had a lovely reception in the Catholic Social Club hall near to the Cathedral. The sad thing was our photographer's camera had a fault which he discovered later. There were no official photographs – all we had were snapshots taken by a few friends.

One little incident I would like to mention is while I was getting dressed for my wedding in Jeanne's mother's house, I received a note written on the back of a cigarette pack from Noel. He was helping to decorate the Hall for the reception. On this bit of card was scribbled the words, 'To the world you are only one, to me you are the world.' These same words, slightly adjusted were written on our (my children's and mine) wreath when he died, 'To the world you were only one, to us you were the world'.

After we were married I remember Noel and I having our fortunes read by a local fortune teller. He told me I would have four children (at the time I was sure he was talking rubbish; it was not in my plans to have any). Noel was told that he would travel abroad and work in a large desert. He also told Noel that he would travel to distant lands and would live to the age of 52. Noel did travel to distant lands. Timbuktu, Mali for one amongst many, and died when he was 51 in Khartoum, Sudan.

We giggled over it at the time and went our way, never knowing how true the prophecy was going to be.

My children were all baptized in Cathedrals, Roger, Diane and Caryl in the Lahore Catholic Cathedral and Lorraine in St Patrick's Cathedral in Karachi. Lahore Cathedral below.

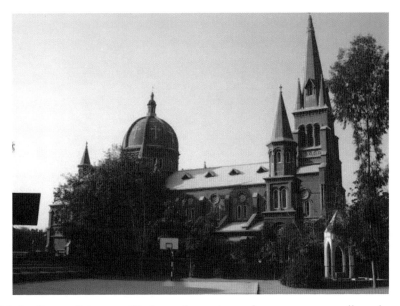

With this heritage of strong willed grandparents, perhaps now you realise why we are all part of a powerful, confident, fun loving, arrogant (if you like) family – blame it on your grandparents on one side of the family at least – both Noel and I were strong, forceful personalities. Perhaps the other side of your parents/grandparents balanced you out a bit.

Some find us as a family, when we are all together, rather intimidating! We are self assured; some would even call us arrogant! But we are a happy lot; full of quick witted humour, love, outgoing, a bit loud and 'in your face' as the cliché says – perhaps too much for the timid, but we do invite people into our inner circle.

We are a close knit, self contained group and what is more, we celebrate being together. Some people fit in perfectly with us and thoroughly enjoy our togetherness. They fit in because they accept us for who we are. There are many that have remained within our close knit circle for years and have become almost a part of our family. One would tend to see the same faces attending our functions; some that have been with our family since they were children. There are those, acquired along life's highways that have become close family and many dear friends. Sadly for some however; and there are the odd few; that seem to feel threatened by our very exuberance and opt to stay on the outside.

As a family group, we are not about to change the way we are. I personally think we are lucky to have each other and to bond the way we do. Of course there are dramatics and upheavals, but that is the way with close knit, strong minded people.

Our strength of personality is deeply ingrained in our roots in our family genes as you will see when reading through this manuscript of family history; that is the part of it that I have knowledge of. There are other branches to your family too and if you need history of those branch lines you will have to trace those for yourselves.

So my darling grandchildren, be happy and proud to be members of this very special group of persons who have been united and tied into a family unit; a unit where all of you, and your extended partners and family, belong and are loved and cherished.

My three girls during winter holidays

I loved attending their little functions of Irish dancing, acrobatics and plays. I remember one show when several children made a pyramid; and guess who was the peak? None other than my Diane! My heart was in my mouth when she climbed up the pyramid to stand on top with her arms spread wide. She held the position for a while and finally the pyramid unscrambled and I breathed a sigh of relief.

Caryl was a cute child, sweet and pretty. All my girls had luscious dark hair with reddish highlights. Diane's hair was a bit lighter than Lorraine's and Caryl's. My three girls had to endure one hundred strokes of a proper bristle brush every night before bed and sometimes in the morning. Caryl gave a lot of trouble while I entangled her hair; screamed, threw tantrums and even shed crocodile tears but I was relentless though I tried very hard to untangle as gently as I could. I hated knots in their hair. I felt that clean, shining; untangled hair was unlikely to get nits and lice! I had a horror of them getting infected; luckily they never did. A lady on a bus once said to me, 'Your children's hair looks so shiny. What do you brush their hair with? Silk?' I have to say that they all had glossy, luxuriant hair. Diane's hair was more like mine and had a different texture to Lorraine's and Caryl's but her hair was abundant and shiny.

Roger did not like water or washing when he was young. He would come to breakfast with a distinct mark on his face in the area that was washed; just in front of each ear. Poor little fellow was always sent back to wash again by me or his grandparents.

We lived in Erith until 1969 when our landlord, who was a supermarket owner, decided he wanted our house for his Manager and I being a trusting person was duped in various traps and had to move out. I was devastated with his threats and did not realize my rights at that time. My Mum said we could come and have a floor in her town house in Surbiton, Surrey. I liked Surbiton and was grateful for somewhere to stay on a temporary basis.

Mum's house was a large town house and the room allotted to us was very large but it was just the one room. By now the children were different and had their own ideas of what they wanted. So this upheaval disturbed them a great deal.

Roger actually had a guinea pig called Henry who was a loved pet in our home. Henry had to come with us to Surbiton and was another occupant or our room. He had his own little sleeping quarters! He was taken out into the garden first thing in the morning, and Mum looked after him in the day.

Whilst in Surbiton the children had to change schools and to my distress they were very unhappy. Diane had just done her 11+ in Erith, Kent and had qualified for a grammar school education. I eventually obtained places for Lorraine and Diane into a Catholic school called Holy Cross. They both hated it. Caryl went to a primary school in Surbiton, which she too hated. Roger would not leave St Josephs and would travel by train to Blackheath, which was quite and ordeal. The fact that my children had been uprooted and were unhappy in their new surroundings was yet another reason for my stress level sky rocketing which eventually lead to a heart attack.

I cannot tell you how upset I was at this happening. The children seemed eventually to accept the inevitable situation and settled into a sort of routine. Henry was fine. I was not. I worked in London and my boss, the Managing Director, who lived in Kingston, picked me up in the morning in his sports car (this was his suggestion). He was a workaholic and would dictate to me in the car so that by the time I arrived at work I had a shorthand notebook filled with work to be done before my work day started. He was a lovely man and I liked working for him and the company. He also droved me home, usually about seven!

What with work pressure and the fact that we all lived in one room stressed me out and I had a heart attack on the May bank holiday in 1970. I was a young forty four and the hospital could not understand why I had such a sever attack. I was quite young and slim. There seemed no reason. This caused big problems for all of us. I was the one that took care of my family as Noel was abroad. Suffice to say it was a hard time for all of us. Noel came home and decided to work in UK. He got a job in Harlow in an IT company called ITT. He worked in a clean area but it was not the kind of work he was used to and I could see that he was not happy.

The good thing that came out of all of this is that we were automatically entitled to a house in Harlow, which was a new town development. I was told how to go about applying.

I was eventually discharged from hospital and Noel and the children had already settled into a new four bedroom house in Harlow. The children were very happy about leaving Surbiton, even though they missed my Mum and their uncles. Noel and the children had sorted out the move and settled in as best they could.

When I arrived I had to rest and all I wanted was to sort the house out the way I wanted to arrange it, but Noel was adamant that I rest. I stayed in the lounge and there was a toilet downstairs so there was no excuse for me to climb stairs, which the doctor had forbidden anyway.

Again there was the problem of school changes which was arranged without too much difficulty. Caryl was in a Primary school, Peterswood and the girls went into Latton Bush which was a Comprehensive school. There were no grammar schools in Harlow.

Caryl came home from school one day and said to me quite seriously, 'How do I become common?' I was shocked and said, 'Why do you want to be common?' She explained that her friends in school said she was 'posh' because she spoke with a posh accent. Apparently she was being ostracized because of this and she wanted to fit in. The funny thing is that she never did develop a Harlow/London accent.

Lorraine and Diane loved their school. It is likely because it was a mixed school whereas they had only been in single sex schools till then.

Roger was a good student and did well in school. He admired the brothers who taught him and decided, quite seriously, that he wanted to be a brother. That meant boarding school training in a seminary atmosphere. I was amazed by this and not too pleased but I went along with it. His Dad was totally against it, but when he came home and talked to Roger, he said he could go ahead.

Roger went off to St Cassians in Kintbury. The school had boarding facilities and was an old stately home. The grounds were picturesque. As one stepped into the entrance hall, one's eye was drawn to a huge print of the painting by Dali of 'Christ of St John of the Cross'. It is such an amazing painting and looked awesome in that fully wood paneled hall. Noel and were taken on a sightseeing tour of the school and were duly impressed with everything we saw. Brother explained to us that Roger would get a sound, classical education as he was training to teach. Since he had shown a desire to follow the De la Salle brotherhood he would automatically be sent to University. My son was very young but the fact that he would have to take a vow of chastity was overwhelming for me as his mother. He seemed very determined and so we followed his wishes.

He was about thirteen when he decided he did not want to stay in St Cassians and be a brother and so he came home and returned to St Joseph's Academy, Blackheath; still with the De la Salle brothers until he was about fifteen. He changed his mind again and told me that he wanted to join the seminary again.

I was embarrassed to speak yet again to Brother Dominic who was head of the seminarians. But he told me not to worry, boys of that age often had changes of heart and that I should go along with what ever he chose. Brother Dominic said he sensed depth of purpose in Roger and that he was not concerned about him.

He was then accepted into a De la Salle boarding house in Cambridge where they studied and lived. He stayed there until he did his A levels then changed his mind yet again and decided he did not want to be a brother. He met lots of pretty girls in Cambridge and when he came home on holiday and decided life outside the seminary would be more the part for him.

I have to say I was relieved and was glad to have him home. He joined his sisters in Laton Bush and finished his A levels there. However he decided not to pursue with studies at University level; he wanted to work. I tried and so did his Dad but it was no use. It is not possible to force an eighteen year old to go to University if he refused to do so. Very unfairly, when he had to do a degree during his working years, he blamed me and said. 'Why didn't you make me go?'

Their teenage years were quite normal or perhaps I should say they were exceptional! They were great kids. I was still working full time in London and travelling from Harlow was even longer than travel from Surbiton. I would return at about seven to find the house tidy and clean. I would cook their evening meal. Sometimes Roger would help prepare vegetables etc before I came home. I did appreciate my children's help.

Caryl did a little to help, but her sisters would argue that point with me. She shared a room with Diane. It was always tidy and neat, because that is the way Diane liked it and so she did all the work. She has always coddled Caryl and still does to this day.

Noel decided that Caryl was not concentrating on study; too much on boys so we chose a very exclusive Boarding school for her in Thornton. It was a Convent and had many students from abroad from wealthy families. It was a beautiful school; another stately home donated to the Convent. She settled in, but we received many reversed charged calls from her everyday. Yet when we visited, the nuns assured us she was doing well. She went to Mass every morning. I could not believe this change in her. I asked the sister if the children were forced to go to Mass and she said, 'Certainly not'. It was entirely up to the students and she said that Caryl was one of the very few who did not miss morning mass. She went to Thornton when she was fourteen and became very unhappy a year later. Noel was determined that she remains in school, but I could not bear her to be so unhappy. We eventually agreed that we would withdraw her and she would go back to Laton Bush.

As they grew older and Roger started dating, we had many parties at home. There would be various age groups who attended our parties. The children had chosen the décor for the house and to say it was garish is an understatement. I wanted it to be their real home and their choices were important. At the time, the seventies, it was a bit of a loud era anyway but everyone seemed to love the ambiance of the house. It became a real party house. I allowed my children a lot of freedom of choice. Right or wrong that is the way it was.

They were good teenagers as teenagers go. Caryl was a bit obstreperous; Roger loved the girls and had many girl friends, Lorraine and Diane too had their favorites of the opposite sex. Caryl seemed to collect boys – sometimes six or seven would call for her, but on many occasions five would be the most common number.

One day while at work, 16 December 1976, I was writing a letter to Noel. I had decided to get a job nearer home and was lucky to find one in Harlow. Roger, who was working in BP by then, arrived at my office door at lunch time. I was always happy to see my son. I stopped writing and greeted him with joy until I saw the look on his face. 'What's the matter? I asked and he said, 'Dad is dead'. I remember this very clearly. It was like a bomb blast. But what happened after that, I am not too clear about. I must have been in shock. Noel was with us on the 14 December 1976 and we had a big party and a sit down meal for about twenty people. He was fine and that is how I remember him. I could not accept it for a many weeks I think.

My next clear memory is of the funeral which was two weeks later as Noel had died in Khartoum of a heart attack on the 15 December. They had to do an autopsy and so could not return his body to England immediately. His death was very sudden. His company took care of everything and paid for the funeral expenses; limousines, catering, the lot. Some of the Americans attended his funeral and many of his working colleagues. I do remember my children always by my side and doing everything. They were my stability in those awful weeks.

I recall as the cavalcade of cars entered the Crematorium that Caryl spoke to me. She said, 'Mum look how beautiful everything is for Dad'. It was one of those sunny winter days when everything seems to sparkle. It is all such a distant and disturbing memory that only little things remain of that awful time. I could barely stand upright during the ceremony and I was aware of being held by Roger and I am not sure who else was near me. One of the girls but I can't remember who.

I, who have such a good memory for detail in lots of ways, cannot remember what and how I behaved after Noel died so suddenly. I know I was totally shaken.

As the years went by, at least two years went by, when Caryl decided to get married at the tender age of seventeen. Both she and her boy friend were seventeen when the wedding took place at my home. I arranged everything and I think it was an occasion that totally exhausted me.

There were issues that I won't go into, but suffice to say that his parents considered them too young, but they refused to listen to any advice and the wedding took place.

The next year Ben was born; my first grandchild.

Well, this is where I will bring my manuscript to an end. Caryl was my first child to marry and have a baby who brought great joy to our family.

Other marriages in our family followed and all of you arrived on this earth to brighten my life. Each one of you brought me extreme joy and gladness. Each one of you lit a bright candle on my altar of glory.

You are my stars, my sunshine and my joy in living. I thank you all for bringing light and love into my world and I thank my children for sharing you with me so very generously.

Your loving Nan

The End

Printed in Great Britain
by Amazon.co.uk, Ltd.,
Marston Gate.